SPORTS CARS

BEEKMAN HOUSE

Louis Weber, C.E.O.
Publications International, Ltd.
7373 N. Cicero Avenue
Lincolnwood, IL 60646

Permission is never granted for commercial purposes.

Manufactured in Yugoslavia
h g f e d c b a

ISBN: 0-517-02734-8

This edition published by Beekman House, Distributed by Crown
Publishers, Inc., 225 Park Avenue South, New York, New York 10003

Library of Congress Catalog Card Number: 90-60057

Picture credits

Chevrolet Motor Division: 34, 35; **Chrysler Corporation:** 60, 61, 62, 63;
Mirco Decet: 21, 23, 56, 91, 92, 93, 94, 96; **Ferrari, Maranello, Italy:**
4-5, 48, 49, 50, 51; **Roland Flessner:** 2, 3, 12, 13, 14, 34, 52, 53, 54,
55, 73, 74, 75, 80, 81, 84; **Alex Gabbard:** 85, 86, 87; **David Gooley:** 42, 43,
44; **Sam Griffith:** 15, 16, 17, 50; **Bert Johnson:** 32; **Bud Juneau:** 27,
28, 29, 33; **Dan Lyons:** 6-7, 8-9; **Mazda Information Bureau:** 67, 68, 69;
Doug Mitchel: 24, 25, 26, 32, 64, 65, 66; **Vince Manocchi:** 30, 31;
Pontiac Motor Division: 76, 77, 78; **Porsche Cars North America, Inc.:**
79, 82, 83; **Joseph Wherry:** 22, 36, 37, 38, 39, 40, 41, 70, 71, 72, 94, 95;
Nicky Wright: 46, 47, 57, 58, 59.

CONTENTS

Shown here: Porsche 944 Turbo. **Front flap:**
MGB. **Rear flap:** Mazda RX-7 convertible.

IN THE DRIVER'S SEAT

Ask ten car enthusiasts to define the term *sports car*, and it's likely you'll hear ten different answers.

In the late Forties and early Fifties, when sports cars first became popular in the U.S., a narrow definition described almost all of them accurately. They were two-seat convertibles with detachable plastic side curtains instead of roll-up windows. Intended for driving fun, and sometimes for high performance, they weren't supposed to be practical.

The term also implied that they were suitable for competition. Ideally, you could drive your sports car to the track, race it, put your trophy in the passenger seat, and drive home.

Large numbers of Americans were introduced to sports cars after World War II, when GIs returning from Europe brought home a strange assortment of British roadsters. People who were used to clumsy, overweight, and dull Detroit cruisers suddenly learned that driving could be great fun. You didn't *have* to slow down for the curves, and blasting along twisting country roads with the wind in your hair was, well, exciting.

These early sports cars were often hard-riding cars with crude weather protection and mechanical technology that was hopelessly outdated even for the late Forties. But they had character, and so did their owners, who happily put up with certain quirks in order to enjoy a special kind of motoring. Many sports-car enthusiasts formed clubs, where they could race their beloved machines and share stories.

But two important trends transformed the sports car into something quite different. First, as the sports-car market expanded, refinement and comfort became

more important. In the U.S., buyers wanted cars that were not only fun to drive, but were also suitable for long trips. While people loved the charm of open-air motoring, they weren't crazy about being caught in a sudden thunderstorm while still struggling to raise a complicated convertible top. Roll-up windows replaced the leaky side curtains, and mechanical parts were brought up to date. Adding a small rear seat for the kids gave young families an excuse to abandon the big sedan and buy a sports car instead.

Meanwhile, the nature of racing was changing. Advancing technology brought race cars that bore little resemblance to a manufacturer's roadgoing models. Modifying a regular production car to be competitive on the track was no longer practical.

So sports cars slowly moved away from the original concept and evolved into what we call *gran turismo* (Italian for "grand touring"), or GT cars. Few cars made today could be called true sports cars, but what's wrong with that? Buyers can choose from a huge array of sporty cars, and manufacturers urgently try to make even 4-door sedans that are fun to drive.

Meanwhile, we invite you to take an exciting look at sports cars from England, Italy, France, Japan, and the U.S. Feast your eyes on—and learn the story behind—many of the great cars, past and present.

Pictured here is a fine example of the Ferrari 328 GTS.

1965-1967 AC SHELBY-COBRA 427

In the early Fifties, AC, a tiny British carmaker, sought to change its reputation for building conservative, antiquated cars. Almost by chance, AC owners Charles and Derek Hurlock were shown a hand-build Tojeiro, a British racing sports car. What attracted the Hurlocks to the Tojeiro design was that the chassis could be produced with little investment, while the body could easily be manufactured at AC's own coachbuilding facility. AC bought the production rights in 1953 and began building the Ace the following year. Power was supplied by an updated version of AC's six-cylinder engine, which traced its heritage to 1919. In 1957, AC added a more modern Bristol six derived from a Thirties BMW design.

However, in 1961 Bristol announced that it would discontinue its six-cylinder engine in favor of a Chrysler Hemi V-8. Just as AC seemed certain to lose its source of engines, American race driver Carroll Shelby proposed shoehorning Ford's forthcoming small-block V-8 into the light and lively Ace. Seventy-five cars were built with the 260-cubic-inch engine, while the next 51 were powered by a 289. Early in 1963, an updated 289-powered Mark II Ace with rack-and-pinion steering was introduced.

The AC Shelby-Cobra had been designed so quickly that most of its chassis, suspension, and general structure was a virtual carryover from the last of the British six-cylinder Aces. After only three years, therefore, a much-revised Cobra, the Mark III, was introduced.

Although the two Mark III models—289 and 427—looked basically alike, they differed in almost every other respect. The most obvious one was the engine of the new 427 model, named for the cubic-inch displacement of its big-block Ford V-8. In addition, it sported a new chassis, new suspension system, and important changes to the bodyshell. With this brutish engine, the Cobra Mark III was sold only in the U.S. Its European cousin, the AC 289, retained the small-block V-8 of the earlier Mark II.

Both Mark IIIs continued with the basic chassis inherited from the AC Ace, though with larger-diameter frame tubes spaced farther apart. Coil springs replaced the old transverse

leaf springs front and rear. Shelby and Ford publicity at the time suggested that this suspension had been computer generated, but actually it was conventionally designed by Bob Negstadt of Shelby-America and Alan Turner of AC. Regardless, the result was more favorable geometry for sharper steering, plus handling that was about as good as this Fifties-vintage chassis could deliver.

With racing in mind—and following the favorite American saying that "there's no substitute for cubic inches"—Shelby's team pursued maximum power by stuffing in the largest V-8 they could. Thus, the small-block 289 V-8 gave way to the massive 427-cid Ford 427, a close relative of the engine used in Ford's NASCAR racers and modified for the GT40 Mark II and Le Mans-winning Mark IV World Manufacturers Championship cars.

But wait. Although the ultimate Cobra was always known as the "427," it seems that many of them were actually built with the low-output 428 engine. So what difference does a cubic inch make? Plenty, for these engines had completely different cylinder dimensions and cylinder-head castings. In short, the 427 was a racing engine, while the 428 was designed for the big Galaxie and Thunderbird passenger cars—considerably heavier than the 427 and more difficult to modify for higher performance.

The Cobra 427 body was similar to that of the Mark III AC 289 and included many common sections. However, wider track dimensions and much fatter tires made it necessary to flare the wheelarches considerably, swelling overall width by seven inches compared to the Mark II shell. This and the burly engine made the 427 a muscular monster that looked as aggressive as it sounded.

In fact, the 427's performance was little short of staggering. Even "customer" cars had 390 horsepower, while race tuning could provide up to 480 bhp and a pavement-peeling 480 lbs/ft of torque. For its three years of production, the Cobra 427 was undoubtedly the wildest and most exciting machine on American roads.

But sales ran down, so production did too, in 1967. For 1968, the Cobra name (which now belonged to Ford,

not Carroll Shelby) began to appear on hopped-up Mustang engines.

In truth, any Cobra, but especially the 427, was too fast for its chassis, and not nearly as refined—or as reliable—as it should have been. Yet because of their rarity and shattering performance, Shelby's high-performance hybrids continued to grow in stature

and to attract the attention of collectors as the years passed. Demand quickly outstripped supply, resulting in a number of Cobra replicas in the Seventies and especially the Eighties. Most employed different and—believe it or not—even cruder chassis designs.

Fortunately, the small but persistent demand for *real* Cobra motoring prompted Brian Angliss and his UK-basked Autokraft company to build "Mark IV" Cobras using surviving original tooling purchased from AC, which Autokraft has since acquired. These cars now have Ford's official sanction, which only goes to show that some legends simply will not be consigned to history.

The Cobra's low build and bulging fenders give it a menacing stance. American race driver and carbuilder Carroll Shelby dropped big Ford V-8s into a British AC roadster body to make the Cobra. Shown here is a Mark III with the monster 427-cubic-inch engine.

SPECIFICATIONS

Engine type	OHV V-8
Displacement	427-428 cid
Horsepower	355-390 @ 5200-5400 rpm
Transmission	4-speed manual
Suspension	all independent
Brakes	front/rear discs
Wheelbase (in.)	90.0
Weight (lbs)	2530
Top speed (mph)	165
0-60 mph (sec)	4.2

The Ford 427-cubic-inch V-8 shown here was a slightly modified racing engine. Fed by four two-barrel carburetors, it was rated at 390 horsepower. Some Cobras were fitted with less powerful 428-cubic-inch engines.

1981-1986 ALFA ROMEO GTV6 2.5

Alfa introduced the Alfetta GT fastback coupe in 1974. The name revived the memory of the Type 158/159 Alfetta racers that enjoyed considerable Grand Prix success in the years just before and after World War II. Alfa changed the name to GTV in 1976, then to Sprint Veloce in 1978. The GT came to the U.S. in 1975 powered by a 1962-cc twincam four, but European versions were available with a choice of 1.6- or 1.8-liter engines as well as the 2.0.

The engines were familiar from previous Alfas, but everything else on the fastback coupe was new. While roomier than previous Alfa coupes, it lacked the older models' grace and flair, nor was it especially practical. It wasn't quite large enough to provide comfortable transportation for four, and wasn't sleek enough to be either a true GT or sports car. And though it looked like it should have been a hatchback, it wasn't. However, these models were the best-handling Alfas to date, thanks to excellent suspension design and near-equal front-to-rear

weight distribution achieved through the use of a rear transaxle.

In most front-engine, rear-wheel-drive cars, the clutch and transmission are bolted directly to the rear of the engine. The Alfetta was unusual in that the clutch, transmission, and rear axle were combined into a single unit (called a transaxle). Moving these heavy drivetrain components to the rear distributes weight more evenly, giving better handling because the lighter front end steers more accurately, while the extra weight over the rear wheels improves traction.

In 1981, this car took on a new image and a superb new V-6 engine to become the GTV6 2.5. Exterior sheetmetal and appearance remained much as before, but structure, suspension, brakes, transaxle, wheels, and tires were all upgraded to cope with the bigger and more potent engine. Sized at 2492 cc, the new V-6 was a single-overhead-cam design with a 60-degree angle between the cylinder banks to assure smooth

running with a minimum of vibration. As on Alfa's four-cylinder powerplants, dome-shaped combustion chambers with a centrally located spark plug promoted rapid and thorough ignition of the fuel mixture.

Both American and European versions were fed by Bosch electronic fuel injection. Rated horsepower was 154 at 5500 rpm with 152 lbs-ft torque at 3200 rpm, sufficient to propel the 2840-pound car from 0-60 mph in 8.4 seconds and on to a top speed of 125 mph. Best of all, when driven hard its refined but urgent wail was sweet music to an enthusiast. With its exotic-looking aluminum castings, it was as much a treat for the eye as for the ear.

The interior wasn't overlooked, either. A tilt wheel, leather upholstery,

Early GTVs had four-cylinder engines, but the car really came alive with Alfa's 2.5-liter V-6. Note the aggressive front spoiler.

9

higher-grade carpeting, and standard air conditioning all made the driver feel good, even if they didn't contribute to performance. A welcome new dashboard placed all the instruments directly in front of the driver; previously, the speedometer and minor gauges were hidden in the center of the dash. However, the ventilation system remained complicated and only marginally effective.

The shift mechanism to the rear-mounted transmission was somewhat soft and rubbery, a penalty of the rear transaxle being placed so far from the shift lever. Although shift quality was much improved on later models, the GTV6 gearbox still didn't like to be rushed. Though slow and heavy at parking speeds, the manual steering was wonderfully precise, and the expertly tuned suspension made fast cornering seem effortless. But those who could ignore—or even learn to enjoy—the GTV6's quirks were rewarded with a most satisfying driving experience.

Fiat purchased Alfa Romeo in 1987. At this writing it is not known if the GTV6, now out of production, will be replaced. While the company concentrates on broadening the appeal of its sedans, it is to be hoped that a new coupe will carry forward a proud tradition.

SPECIFICATIONS

Engine type	SOHC V-6
Displacement	154.8 cid/ 2492 cc
Horsepower	154 @ 5500 rpm
Transmission	5-speed manual
Suspension	all independent
Brakes	front/rear discs
Wheelbase (in.)	94.5
Weight (lbs)	2840
Top speed (mph)	125
0-60 mph (sec)	8.4

The GTV6 looks like it's moving even when standing still. This high-performance version includes a special front spoiler and side extensions. The hood bulge is needed to fit Alfa's six-cylinder engine, which looks as good as it sounds.

1955-1990 ALFA ROMEO GIULIETTA SPIDER/ GIULIA SPIDER

In the Fifties, if you wanted the joys of open-air motoring in a small, reasonably priced two-seat sports car, you had to earn the privilege. Raising or lowering the top was clumsy and time consuming, as was wrestling with the removable side curtains. And after all that, the car still leaked if you drove in the rain.

But in 1955, Italian sports-car maker Alfa Romeo changed all that. The new Giulietta Spider featured genuine roll-up windows and an easy-to-fold convertible top with effective weather sealing. Designed by Battista Pinin Farina, the graceful-looking roadster suddenly made those British sports cars look hopelessly old fashioned.

The 1290-cc engine was as modern and up-to-date as the cars it powered. The block was lightweight aluminum and featured cast-iron cylinder liners for durability. Double overhead camshafts allowed the spark plugs to be placed centrally in dome-shaped combustion chambers, promoting more rapid and complete burning of the air/fuel mixture. The valves—two per cylinder—were angled to ease the flow of intake and exhaust gases. At first only one state of tune was available, yielding 80 horsepower at 6300 rpm, but 1956 brought a 90-horsepower Veloce version.

For 1962, the car was renamed Giulia and a 1.6-liter engine (actually 1570 cc) replaced the 1.3. Rated at 104 horsepower at 6200 rpm, this engine was at first the Giulias' only real distinction aside from minor trim changes. But the extra displacement and resulting increase in power at lower engine speeds made for a more pleasurable car that was easier to drive. A 5-speed all-synchromesh gearbox replaced the previous 4-speed.

By 1963, a new Giulia sedan and Sprint were on sale with all-new bodywork and more sophisticated suspension. The 1966 Geneva show saw the debut of a new small Alfa convertible. Dubbed "Duetto," this design, again by Battista Pininfarina (spelled as one word since 1961) was inspired by a styling exercise seen at Geneva in 1959. The rounded front and rear, connected by a wide full-length bodyside groove, generated decidedly mixed feelings among Alfa enthusiasts. Pininfarina also built the production Duetto bodies under contract.

Giulia displacement swelled to 1779 cc in 1969, but Alfa called the cars "1750." This engine further aided the small Alfas' overall flexibility, though horsepower and torque were not greatly increased. The Duetto was now simply called Spider. In 1971 the rounded rear styling gave way to a rather abruptly chopped tail, a change many felt was not in keeping with the classic harmony of the original design.

Because of American exhaust emissions standards and other bureaucratic requirements, no Alfas were marketed in the U.S. for 1972. When the 1973 models appeared, the Giulia engine had been further enlarged, to 1962 cc, for a revised group of 115-series 2000 models. Spica mechanical fuel injection replaced the dual Weber carburetors for the American market in the interest of improved running characteristics and cleaner exhaust.

An interesting development for 1980 was the adoption of variable valve timing. Let's take a moment to understand how it works. As the names imply, the intake valves open to admit the air/fuel mixture into the cylinders, while the exhaust valves allow the burned gases to be expelled. The valves are opened and closed by tapered "bumps," called lobes, on a rotating camshaft. The size and shape of these lobes determine how far each valve is opened, and how long it stays open. In a conventional engine, the valves open and close at the same intervals regardless of engine speed. The problem is that for good power output at higher engine speeds, the exhaust valve should open before the intake valve has closed; this is called overlap. But too much overlap makes the engine run poorly at low speeds, wasting fuel and increasing exhaust emissions. Commonly, engineers must compromise the engine's performance, sacrificing either high-speed power or low-speed smoothness, ease of driving, and emissions control.

But if valve overlap could be changed automatically, an engine could run strongly and efficiently at low speeds without hurting performance at higher rpms. Alfa engineers designed a camshaft with a special gear that could increase or decrease overlap by rotating the camshaft slightly. An electrical signal from the engine's ignition system "tells" the camshaft to increase or decrease the overlap, while the actual adjustment is accomplished by varying oil pressure inside the gear assembly. Alfa's system is among the first modern applications for variable valve timing, and similar systems are likely to see much wider use by a number of carmakers in the coming years.

For 1982 U.S. models, the mechanical injection was shelved in favor of a Bosch electronic system, in combination with a state-of-the-art electronic ignition. For 1985, a small computer was employed for more precise control of the variable valve timing.

Despite these up-to-date features, the Spider cannot disguise its age. Having served faithfully for twenty-five years, it's due for an honorable retirement. Latest word is that an all-new Spider will be introduced in 1993 to satisfy a new generation of enthusiasts.

The Alfa Spider's classic styling dates from the mid-Sixties, and still looks remarkably fresh. The front and rear spoilers were added in the early Eighties. Shown here is a 1986 Spider Veloce.

This 1986 Spider Veloce features leather upholstery and air conditioning. The convertible top is easy to raise and lower.

SPECIFICATIONS

Engine type	DOHC inline-4
Displacement	78.7 cid/1290 cc to 119.7 cid/ 1962 cc
Horsepower	80 @ 6300 rpm to 132 @ 5500 rpm
Transmission	4- and 5-speed manual
Suspension	independent front, live rear axle
Brakes	front/rear drums, front/ rear discs
Wheelbase (in.)	88.6
Weight (lbs)	1936-2300
Top speed (mph)	115
0-60 mph (sec)	10.6-12.2

1971-1985 ALPINE-RENAULT A310

The first Alpine-Renaults date from the Fifties. Designed by Jean Redele and built by his company in Dieppe, France, they were fast but fragile rear-engine coupes with fiberglass bodies and Renault mechanical parts. But these were cramped little two-seaters more suited to racing or European rallying than daily driving.

A new model was long overdue by l971, and Alpine-Renault surprised everyone that year with the new A3l0, a larger, more spacious, and much more practical machine. It was so different from the older models that both continued in production for a number of years.

The graceful, modern A310 followed the familiar Alpine-Renault formula in many ways. The engine was placed in the rear, and a fiberglass body was attached to a steel chassis. Compared with the earlier A110, it was longer, wider, and far roomier. It had a small rear seat.

The original A310 used the most powerful Renault production engine then available, an overhead-valve 1.6 liter four-cylinder. The engine's 127 horsepower gave the French coupe a 131-mph top speed.

Unfortunately, sales did not meet expectations. Quality-control problems on early A310s kept some potential customers away, while others were turned off by its rear-engine layout. (Rear-engine cars can be very tricky to control in fast cornering.) When the first Arab oil embargo in 1973-74 made buyers even more reluctant, Alpine-Renault found itself in serious financial trouble. But Renault came to the rescue by buying the firm, and Alpine has seen steady expansion ever since.

Late in 1976, a faster V-6-powered A310 was added. Developed by Peugeot, Renault, and Volvo, the engine was used in many cars made by the three companies. Made of light-weight aluminum and featuring single overhead camshafts, the V-6 suited the A310's character very well. Its 150 bhp pushed top speed up to about 137 mph, making this the world's quickest rear-engine production car apart from the Porsche 911.

Exactly 2334 four-cylinder A310s had been built in five years, but the new V-6 sold better. Other improvements helped: A 5-speed became standard in 1979, and the interior was upgraded in late 1982. Most A310s were sold in Europe, but a few made it to the U.S. Production continued at Dieppe until 1985, when the A310 gave way to the new GTA.

The A310 sold well by Alpine-Renault standards, and the small factory was kept busy to the end. Clearly, Renault judged the A310 a success, for the GTA that replaced it was very much the same type of car.

The Alpine-Renault A310 was a rear-engine sports car with a fiberglass body. A small rear seat was suitable for children. Early models used Renault four-cylinder engines, but later cars were V-6 powered.

SPECIFICATIONS

Engine type	OHV inline-4, SOHC V-6
Displacement	98 cid/1605 cc, 162.5 cid/ 2664 cc
Horsepower	127 @ 6250 rpm to 150 @ 6000 rpm
Transmission	4- and 5-speed manuals
Suspension	all independent
Brakes	front disk/rear drum (4-cyl.), front/rear disc (V-6)
Wheelbase (in.)	89.4
Weight (lbs)	2075-2240
Top speed (mph)	131-137
0-60 mph (sec)	7.5-8.1

The car shown here is a later-model V-6 with more aggressive detail styling. The engine is the 1.6-liter Renault four-cylinder, which was rated at 127 horsepower.

1985-1990
ALPINE-RENAULT GTA

Renault produced the Alpine-Renault A310 V-6 for more than eight years before fielding a stunning replacement. Although this new GTA is similar in many ways, it has a lot that's completely new. It's certainly the most professional Alpine-Renault yet. Where the A310 had been created inexpensively by Jean Redele's company, the GTA was designed by Renault itself, using computer-assisted design techniques. Also, while the A310 was intended only to be sold in Europe, Renault planned to export the GTA, particularly to the U.S.

Let's look at the similarities first. The A310 used a steel frame, with the engine carried behind and driving the rear wheels. Its fiberglass body could seat four. The GTA retains this basic package but is larger and more modern. The front and rear axles are three inches farther apart, and the car is four inches wider and two inches taller.

The GTA boasts an improved structure. Instead of using an entirely separate body bolted to the steel frame, the fiberglass panels are bonded, or glued, to the chassis. Since the body and chassis are a single unit, the assembly is more rigid.

Compared with the A310, the GTA's styling was very carefully studied to improve aerodynamics. While the A310 also featured sloping glass headlamp covers, a low front air dam (or chin spoiler), and a built-in rear spoiler, the GTA's styling was shaped in a wind tunnel. Renault claims that air drag is the lowest of any production car in the world.

Mechanically, the GTA is a further evolution of the A310. Power is still provided by the Peugeot-Renault-Volvo V-6, but two versions are now used. The basic GTA carries a 2849-cc carbureted engine good for 160 bhp at 5750 rpm. But the big news was availability of the 200-bhp 2458-cc turbocharged version from the big Renault 25 sedan, which gives the GTA a top speed of 150 mph. A 5-speed manual transmission is standard; as in the A310, automatic is not available. To tame the tail-heavy handling (front/rear weight distribution is 39/63 percent), Renault mounts larger tires on the rear than on the front. Disc brakes are used on all four wheels.

Although the GTA feels like a much better car than the A310, its handling still occasionally suffers from the rear-engine layout. Lifting off the gas pedal in tight corners can result in a spin, as it does on many Porsche 911s. And make no mistake: The GTA, especially the Turbo, is as fast as it looks. Yet because of the rear-engine position, it's surprisingly quiet when driven fast. There's also no doubt that it has more interior space than its obvious rivals. Renault believes they've produced a better car than the 911, though only time will tell.

Sad to say, the GTA won't be sold in North America after all, even though it was designed to meet strict U.S. safety and exhaust emissions standards. The reason, of course, is the 1987 Chrysler Corporation buyout of Renault's stake in American Motors.

So the GTA has been locked out of the U.S. market, and it's too bad. Cars like this make life more interesting for serious drivers, and American enthusiasts will be that much poorer for lack of the GTA.

The GTA featured smoother looks and better aerodynamics than the A310 that it replaced, but it was actually two inches taller. Power came from one of two V-6s.

SPECIFICATIONS

Engine type	SOHC V-6, naturally aspirated and turbocharged
Displacement	174 cid/2849 cc, 150 cid/2458 cc (turbo)
Horsepower	160 @ 5750 rpm, 200 @ 5750 rpm (turbo)
Transmission	5-speed manual
Suspension	all independent
Brakes	front/rear discs
Wheelbase (in.)	92.1
Weight (lbs)	2620
Top speed (mph)	149 (turbo)
0-60 mph (sec)	6.3 (turbo)

Alpine-Renaults have long been popular with racers. Both non-turbo and turbocharged Peugeot-Renault-Volvo V-6 engines are offered. GTAs are not sold in the U.S.

1953-1967 AUSTIN-HEALEY 100/4, 100 SIX, & 3000

America emerged from World War II hungry for cars. Car production had been suspended for four years in order to make military equipment. And although Americans eagerly bought almost anything with wheels, a new market was taking shape.

The car was becoming more than just transportation; it was a means of expression. Dull sedans were okay for carrying the family or getting groceries, but many people wanted more. They wanted cars with style, flair, and character, cars that were fun to drive. What could be more perfect than cruising in a low-slung sports car with the wind in your hair?

The sports car may not have been invented in England, but it found a perfect breeding ground there. And Donald Healey bred some of the best.

In the two decades before World War II, Healey gained fame as a rally driver in England and throughout Europe. After the war, he began to build sports cars under his own name using mechanical parts from the larger manufacturers. These early Healeys were relatively expensive and were built in small numbers; most were sold in Europe.

Many Americans had their first taste of sports cars with models like this Austin-Healey 100/4. The windshield could be tilted back for real wind-in-the-hair motoring.

By the early Fifties, Healey wanted to build an up-to-date, more affordable sports car to tap the huge American market. His new car would be less expensive than a Jaguar, while faster and more modern than the outdated MG. Healey approached Leonard Lord, managing director of British Motor Corporation (BMC), with his idea. Lord was keenly interested, partly because his slow-selling Austin Atlantic left him with more engines and transmissions than he could use. Healey's proposed sports car would be simple, rugged, and easy to build.

Lord approved the plan, and Healey's design team came up with a sleek, graceful prototype. Shown at the 1952 London Motor Show, the car created a sensation. In 1953, the Austin-Healey 100/4 was introduced, powered by a 2660-cc four-cylinder engine. Exports to the U.S. soon followed.

Since BMC was planning to stop producing the four-cylinder engine, a trip to the company parts bin yielded a 2639-cc six-cylinder to replace it in 1956. In other changes, the distinctive shell-shaped grille became an oval, and the folding windshield was replaced by fixed glass. To satisfy American buyers, who don't often take kindly to two-seaters, the wheelbase was stretched by two inches and two small rear seats were added. The name became Austin-Healey 100 Six.

Despite the two extra cylinders, the 100 Six was actually slower than the four-cylinder model it replaced. The Six produced more horsepower (102 instead of 90), but its 300 extra pounds canceled out the power advantage.

An upgraded model, called the 3000, was introduced in the spring of 1959. At first, the 3000 was little more than a 100 Six with a bigger engine and better brakes. The engine was now sized at 2912 cc and yielded 124 horsepower. The front drum brakes were replaced by discs. The 3000 was available as a two-seater or as a 2+2.

Two years later, BMC announced the 3000 Mark II. The only significant change was the use of three carburetors instead of two. Even though rated horsepower increased to 132, acceleration didn't improve. The three-carb setup proved so tricky to tune that it was dropped after only a year.

At the end of summer 1962, the Mark II became Mark II Sports Convertible. BMC added a slightly more curved windshield, and roll-up windows replaced the removable side curtains. Another welcome improvement was a new easy-to-fold convertible top. The two-seater was discarded and all 3000s were now 2+2s. All in all, the new 3000 was a more modern and practical package.

Another major revision in the spring of 1964 was the advent of the 3000 Mark III. Although engine size stayed

the same, horsepower increased to 148, good for a top speed of about 120 mph. A restyled dashboard featured wood paneling, and a center console was added between the seats. Later in the year, a "Phase II" version arrived with modified rear suspension.

By the mid-Sixties, the 3000 was beginning to look old-fashioned. Faced by new U.S. safety and emissions regulations, BMC decided that the modifications required to meet them weren't worth the money. So, except for a single car assembled in 1968, production stopped at the end of 1967.

It's easy to forget that these Austin-Healeys were, in a sense, more American than British. They were designed for the American market, and almost 90 percent were sold here. Now, they serve as a pleasant reminder of a vanished era.

SPECIFICATIONS

Engine type	OHV inline-4, OHV inline-6
Displacement	162.3 cid/2660 cc, 177 cid/ 2912 cc
Horsepower	90 @ 4000 rpm, 102-117 @ 4600- 4750 rpm
Transmission	3- and 4-speed manuals
Suspension	independent front/live rear axle
Brakes	front/rear drums
Wheelbase (in.)	90.0, 92.0
Weight (lbs)	2015-2435
Top speed (mph)	103-111
0-60 mph (sec)	10.3-12.9

Gentle curves and wire wheels gave the Austin-Healey a classic look. Early models came with removable side curtains, but genuine roll-up windows were added in 1962. The Austin-Healey was designed for the American market, and almost 90 percent were sold in the U.S.

1958-1961 AUSTIN-HEALEY SPRITE

Few cars have been more right for their time than the original Austin-Healey Sprite, the beloved "Bugeye." It was conceived to fill an obvious market gap that existed by the time the genuinely small sporting MGs, the Midgets of the Thirties and Forties, had evolved into the larger and costlier MGA of the Fifties.

British Motor Corporation (BMC) chairman Sir Leonard Lord rarely missed a commercial trick, and invited the Healey family to design a small, back-to-basics sports car that would appeal to a different market than the popular MGA. Since this collaboration had already led to the Austin-Healey 100, which was selling very well in the U.S., Lord was convinced that the new small Healey would enjoy similar success. He was right.

Donald Healey and sons went to work on the new car, though their creation was finalized by MG and put into production beginning in mid-1958. BMC delved into its big box of registered trademarks for the model name, which had graced a Riley sports car of the Thirties. (The Nuffield Organisation had acquired Riley in 1938, then joined Austin in 1952 to form BMC.)

Built on an 80-inch wheelbase, the Sprite was tiny by the standards of its day (and ours, too) though larger and heavier than Thirties Midgets. Alfa Romeo and Fiat had already produced unit-construction sports cars (both on shortened mass-market sedan platforms) but the Sprite was the first British sports car to abandon old-fashioned body-on-frame construction. Although it was a bare-bones two-seat roadster, at 1460 pounds it wasn't all that light for its size.

To keep the Sprite structure as simple and rigid as possible, the Healeys omitted an external trunklid; luggage was loaded through the cockpit by folding down the seats. Front sheetmetal—hood, fenders, and surrounding panels—lifted up as a unit, giving easy access to the engine and front suspension. Instead of roll-up windows, Sprite used side curtains—transparent plastic mounted in a frame which could be attached to the doors. The soft top was a characteristically British design which was difficult and time-consuming to raise or lower, though an optional

bolt-on hardtop was offered soon after introduction.

The protruding headlamps gave the Sprite a "bugeye" or "frogeye" look, which explains the nicknames that persist to this day. This appearance distinction was quite accidental. Retractable lights had been planned but were canceled at the last minute as too costly, by which time it was too late to change the styling.

Cost considerations also dictated off-the-shelf running gear and chassis components, a mixture of items from two small BMC family sedans. The Morris Minor 1000 donated its rack-and-pinion steering, while the Sprite's

4-speed gearbox, firmed-up front suspension, and BMC A-series four-cylinder engine came from the Austin A35.

The result was a perky little car with enormous character. With its simple rear suspension, the Bugeye could be unstable in corners, but since the steering was so responsive—and top speed only 80 mph—it rarely got away from you. And because it could be flung about with abandon, the Sprite was perfect for slaloms, gymkhanas, and other competition, and demand from weekend warriors soon prompted all sorts of engine and handling upgrades from aftermarket

sources. Much-modified Sprites, with front-disc brakes, high-performance engines, and smoothed-out bodywork competed with distinction against far larger and more powerful machines at places like Sebring and Daytona.

Mechanical sturdiness and race-and-ride versatility helped sales, but price was the big factor. At about $1500 new, the Sprite was cheap—$1000 or so less than an MGA and Triumph TR3--and an outstanding buy. But the car wouldn't stay in production long: just three years and near 49,000 units. Its successor, the Sprite Mark II of 1961 (also cloned for a new MG Midget), was much the same car with

extra features and more conventional, square-rigged styling.

But Len Lord's bargain-basement roadster had done its job, teaching an entire generation what affordable sports-car motoring was all about. While it's likely that fewer than half the original Bugeyes survive today, it's almost possible to build a new one from scratch, so numerous are the reproductions of virtually everything—mechanical parts, body panels, trim, the works. It may be surprising that such a simple, inexpensive car can inspire such long-lived affection, but then, the Bugeye was much more than the sum of its humble parts.

SPECIFICATIONS

Engine type	OHV inline-4
Displacement	57.9 cid/948 cc
Horsepower	43 @ 5200 rpm
Transmission	4-speed manual
Suspension	independent front/live rear axle
Brakes	front/rear drums
Wheelbase (in.)	80.0
Weight (lbs)	1460
Top speed (mph)	80
0-60 mph (sec)	20.9

The Austin-Healey Sprite was smaller and considerably less expensive than other British sports cars of its day. Power came from a 1.0-liter Austin four-cylinder engine. Top speed was 80 mph.

The bulging headlights earned the nicknames "bugeye" and "frogeye." Retractable headlights had been planned, but were abandoned for cost reasons. The hood and fenders opened together for good service access.

1968-1977 BMW 2800CS, 2.5CS & 3.0CS/CSi/CSL

BMW's great sales success in the 1970s and '80s was partly due to its introduction of a new family of overhead-camshaft engines in the Sixties. The first of these engines appeared in late 1961 to power a "New Generation" 1500 sedan. Since then, the engine has been built in both four- and six-cylinder versions. It has varied in displacement from the initial 1.5 liters to as much as 3.5 liters, and remains in production today.

As this engine grew, the original "New Generation" sedan became more powerful, being offered in 1600 (1.6-liter), 1800 (1.8-liter), and 2000 (2.0-liter) models. But the quick little sedan was rather boxy looking, so in 1965, BMW decided to build a version with a sleek new body. The result was a streamlined coupe called the 2000CS.

While the new coupe was much better looking than the sedan, it was given a front-end treatment that seemed somewhat awkward. And although the 2.0-liter four-cylinder engine had been pumped up to 120 horsepower, it just didn't provide the performance promised by the coupe's sporty looks.

But it didn't take long for BMW to fix these flaws. In 1968, the carmaker brought out a six-cylinder version of the coupe called the 2800CS. Besides being more powerful, it also had a longer, redesigned front end that transformed the car from ugly duckling to beautiful swan. The results, seen on these pages, speak for themselves.

Even better, the 2800CS was now as fast as it looked. The new 2.8-liter six-cylinder engine delivered 170 horsepower, and was much smoother than the four-cylinder engine it replaced. Furthermore, with all-independent coil-spring suspension and front disc brakes, the chassis was more than able to hold up its end of the performance bargain. With the 2800CS, BMW finally had a great-looking coupe that could fly down the straightaways, and stick like glue in the corners.

Although BMW did the design work and provided the engine and chassis, both the 2000CS and 2800CS were actually built in Austria by a company called Karmann. Besides providing the beautiful skin, Karmann also gave the coupes a comfortable interior trimmed with top-quality materials. Back seat room was rather tight, however, resulting in what is called "2+2" seating—meaning that two adults could sit in front, but the rear seat was only large enough for two children to be comfortable.

BMW offered the handsome coupe for nearly ten years—a long model run by today's standards, but about average for the German carmaker at that time. However, some minor changes were made along the way. In 1971, the engine was enlarged to 3.0 liters, and the car's name was changed to 3.0CS. (BMW began using the engine's size in liters instead of cubic centimeters to name all its cars during this period). Soon after, fuel-injection replaced the carburetors on the 3.0-liter engine, and the name changed again to 3.0CSi. The displacement increase added 10 horsepower, and fuel injection added 20 more, so the already fast coupe got faster still. On both cars, stronger disc brakes were used at the rear instead of drum brakes to offset the increased power.

Also appearing in '71 was a stripped-down racing version of the CS coupe. Called the 3.0CSL, it used lighter-weight aluminum instead of steel in many body panels. It had the carbureted engine at first, but in late

This 2800CS is powered by a 2.8-liter six-cylinder engine rated at 170 horsepower. The design and chassis components came from BMW, but cars were assembled at Karmann in Austria.

1972 it got fuel injection as well as a slightly larger engine. A year later, displacement was increased again for a third CSL, which was available with a front spoiler and shark-like fins in the rear. The CSLs won a number of road races both in the U.S. and Europe, and even won the European Touring Car Championship several times.

But not all the coupes got bigger, more powerful engines. In mid-1974, a 2.5-liter version of the CS was introduced. BMW wanted to offer a less expensive, more fuel efficient car during the "Energy Crisis" that was going on in the U.S. However, only 844 were built during its one year of production, making the 2.5CS one of the rarer BMWs of modern times.

While all the CS coupes are fast, some are faster than others. Although the 2800CS could reach 128 mph, the injected 3.0CSi could do nearly 140 mph, completing the 0-60-mph dash in just 7.5 seconds. This kind of performance, along with styling that has held up amazingly well over the years, makes owning a CS coupe a rare pleasure indeed.

SPECIFICATIONS

Engine type	SOHC inline-6
Displacement	152 cid/2494 cc to 192 cid/ 3153 cc
Horsepower	150 to 206 bhp @ 6000 to 6600 rpm
Transmission	4-speed manual or 3-speed automatic (except CSL)
Suspension	all independent
Brakes	front/rear discs (rear drums on 2800CS)
Wheelbase (in.)	103.3
Weight (lbs)	2775-3085
Top speed (mph)	139 (3.0CSi)
0-60 mph (sec)	7.5 (3.0CSi)

The 3.0CSL was a stripped-down coupe with lightweight aluminum body panels. This 1973 model features bizarre fins on the trunklid and a front "chin" spoiler. CSLs won road races both in Europe and in the U.S.

1963-1967 CHEVROLET CORVETTE STING RAY

To many car buffs, the early Sting Ray is regarded as the best Corvette ever built. It carried the most radical changes yet seen in the Corvette's 10-year history, proving to be a styling showpiece and an engineering masterpiece.

Introduced for 1963, the Sting Ray took both its name and general shape from Chevrolet's late-Fifties Stingray racer, and was quite unlike any other car on the road. Apart from four wheels and two seats, the only things it shared with the '62 Corvette were steering, front suspension, engines, and fiberglass bodywork. Most everything else was changed—and for the better.

Where previous Corvettes had been rather rounded and fat-looking, the new Sting Ray was sleek and smooth. But the big news was independent rear suspension, which gave the new car much more stable handling and a smoother ride. A first for a modern U.S. production car, it was designed by Zora Arkus-Duntov, an engineer who had long been an important member of the Corvette development team. Also new was a transverse-mounted rear leaf spring that went side-to-side across the car, connecting at each end near the rear wheels. Earlier Corvettes (and most other cars, for that matter) used two leaf springs, one for each rear wheel, that went front-to-back rather than side-to-side. This transverse spring arrangement must have worked well, because it's still being used on Corvettes today.

As for the styling, it looks great even now. You can imagine how fresh it looked back in 1963. Part of this was due to the fact that previous Corvettes had only been available as convertibles. But the Sting Ray could be had either as a convertible or a fastback coupe, so the new coupe was something new indeed. The 1963 coupe came with a center bar that divided the rear window, and this model became known as the "split-window coupe." Later versions of the Sting Ray did away with the dividing bar and went to a one-piece rear window, leaving

The clean-looking, sharp-edged styling of the 1963 Corvette helped nearly double sales. The coupe was new for '63; previous 'Vettes were sold only as convertibles.

the split-window coupe a one-year model—and highly prized because of it.

The Sting Ray quickly proved the fastest and most roadable Corvette yet—and the most popular: 1963 sales were nearly twice the record '62 total. Although performance and styling certainly played a part in this, the new car also offered luxury options such as leather upholstery, power steering, power brakes, AM/FM radio, and air conditioning. No longer was the inside of a Corvette an uncomfortable, drafty place to be.

Over the next four years, the Sting Ray became even more powerful, and some say, better looking. Appearance was actually changed very little, but some of the exterior details were cleaned up, making the car look even more streamlined. The "small-block" 327-cid V-8 engine was standard throughout this model run, and in 1964, fuel injection was fitted to an optional engine that produced 375 horsepower. A 396-cid "big-block" V-8 with 425 horsepower was offered in 1965, and an even bigger 427-cid, 435 horsepower version came out in 1966. Although the standard engines made the Corvette plenty quick, any of these

optional engines could really make it fly. One magazine reported that a 435 horsepower Corvette could do the 0-60-mph sprint in 4.8 seconds and top 140 mph. And if that wasn't enough, Chevrolet even made a handful of Corvettes with a 560 horsepower engine! This was the famous L88—very rare today, since only 20 were built.

In 1968 the Corvette was restyled again and looked completely different. But in the hearts of car lovers everywhere, the original Sting Ray will always be a favorite. It was—and is—very special, the kind of car that happens only once in a lifetime.

SPECIFICATIONS

Engine type	OHV V-8
Displacement	327 cid/5359 cc to 427 cid/ 6997 cc
Horsepower @ rpm	250 bhp @ 4400 rpm to 435 bhp @ 5800 rpm
Transmission	3- or 4-speed manual, 2-speed automatic
Suspension	all independent
Brakes	front/rear drums (1963-64); front/ rear discs (1965-67)
Wheelbase (in.)	98.0
Weight (lbs)	3050-3270
Top speed (mph)	105-150
0-60 mph (sec)	4.8-8.0

The '63 Corvette coupe featured a split rear window, which was replaced by one-piece glass for 1964. All the Corvettes were fast, but some could sprint from 0-60 mph in less than five seconds.

1984-1989 CHEVROLET CORVETTE

By 1982, Corvette fans were getting restless. Since its birth in 1953, the Corvette had gone through five major styling changes (called "generations"). The first generation lasted through 1955, the second ran through 1957, and the third carried on until the Sting Ray (fourth generation) came out in '63. For 1968, the fifth generation appeared, and that one was still with us in 1982—15 years later. It was time for a change.

Chevrolet had been promising that a new Corvette was in the works, and after waiting so long, people expected great things from this latest version. Many expected that the new car would emerge as a 1983 model, since that would be the 30th anniversary of the first Corvette—fitting for an all-new design. But although the new car was introduced in 1983, it wasn't a 30th-anniversary edition.

The "old" 1982 model continued to be sold through the end of that year, and Chevrolet chose to bring out the new Corvette in early '83 as the first

1984 model. Because of this, there actually was no 1983 Corvette, and many diehard fans were disappointed. But they were not disappointed for long.

The sixth-generation Corvette arrived with an angular, sweeping shape that was quite different from the '82's curvy profile. Some people liked the new design, while others thought it was bland, but nobody ever called it ugly.

In place of the T-tops offered in '82, the '84 came with a full Targa roof, and this change required a new chassis design as well. T-tops have two removable panels, one above each side of the passenger compartment. When the roofs are taken off, a support bar remains in the middle that adds stiffness to the body structure. Targa roofs, however, are fully open over the passenger area when the roof is removed. To maintain body stiffness, the floor must be strengthened. In the case of the Corvette, this was done by adding a strong steel "tunnel" that ran

between the seats from the front of the passenger compartment to the back. Commonly known as a "backbone" chassis, it was a design that had long been used by Lotus, an English carmaker.

The engine in the '84 version was the same 205-horsepower V-8 as was used in 1982. However, where only an automatic transmission was offered before, the new car was also available with an unusual "4+3 Overdrive" manual transmission. It worked like a normal four-speed, except that a second ratio was available for second, third, and fourth gears. In gentle or moderate driving, the engine computer automatically selected the "taller" ratio to reduce engine speed and improve fuel mileage.

Weight saving was also important, so the '84 made use of more lightweight

The sixth-generation Corvette's shape was more angular and less rounded than earlier models. This 1985 Corvette has the one-piece Targa removable roof panel.

materials than any other Corvette. The suspension system is a good example. Many pieces that would normally be made of steel were made from lighter-weight aluminum instead. And the transverse leaf springs, used both front and rear, were actually made of plastic. All told, this helped make the new car 250 pounds lighter than the '82, which aided both performance and economy. Handling was likewise helped by huge tires that were about the widest found on any American car.

For 1985, the Corvette gained 25 horsepower and an improved suspension system. A convertible version, last offered for 1975, reappeared for 1986, and 1987s were treated to another 10 horsepower. In 1988, horsepower went up again, bringing the total to 245, and even larger tires were offered.

For 1989, the 4+3 manual transmission was replaced by a six-speed. In gentle driving, the shift lever moved from first gear directly into fourth, but all six ratios were available with a heavier foot on the gas pedal.

But the biggest news is yet to come. For 1990, Chevrolet introduced the ZR-1, a 375-horsepower monster that has already proven itself to be the fastest Corvette yet. And who knows what's coming next.

SPECIFICATIONS

Engine type	OHV V-8
Displacement	350 cid/5735 cc
Horsepower	205 @ 4200 rpm to 245 @ 4000 rpm
Transmission	"4+3" overdrive manual or 4-speed automatic, 6-speed manual
Suspension	all independent
Brakes	front/rear discs
Wheelbase (in.)	96.2
Weight (lbs)	3190-3280
Top speed (mph)	150+
0-60 mph (sec)	5.8

A 1986 Indianapolis 500 pace car replica. **Inset:** The interior of the 1986 Corvette roadster.

1961-1969 DATSUN 1500 SPORTS/1600/2000

Remember the cars the Japanese used to build back in the 1960s? If you don't (or even if you do), it's interesting to go back and take a look at some of them. For one thing, you'll find that the products of Honda, Toyota, and Nissan were not always the sleek, comfortable cars we see today. Looking back will also give you an idea of how far the Japanese industry has come— and how quickly. Nissan's first sports cars are a good example.

First of all, Nissan was not always known by that name. The company built its first car, called the DAT, in 1914, and the cars later took on the name Datsun. However, the company that built them was the Nissan Motor Corporation. Cars that were shipped to the U.S. continued to carry the Datsun name until the early 1980s, at which time the company started calling them Nissans.

Datsun began building sports cars as early as 1952, but the first ones that sold in large numbers came in 1959. These carried the odd name "Fairlady," but were also known as the S211. It was a two-seat convertible (called a "roadster") that was powered by a small, 1.2-liter, 60-horsepower engine. Because of this, it was much slower than other sports cars of the day. But better things weren't long in coming.

In 1961, Datsun brought out a new sports car with a more powerful 1.5-liter engine. Called the Fairlady 1500 or SP310, it looked like the cars shown on these pages. It also looked like the MG roadsters that came out about that time, and some people thought Datsun had copied the English cars. But in fact, the SP310 was actually brought out first.

More grown up and civilized than the S211, the SP310 offered both better performance and better styling. It had a clean, slab-sided body, with headlights that were "scooped" into the front fenders. At first it was a three-seater, with a single sideways-facing rear bucket seat, but that feature was dropped by 1963.

Mechanically, it was also much like other sports cars of the day. It had a separate frame with coil spring front suspension, leaf springs in the rear, and drum brakes all around. The powertrain was also rather ordinary: a 71-horsepower inline four-cylinder engine and a 4-speed manual transmission.

As was Japanese custom even in those long-ago days, the Fairlady 1500 was fully equipped and priced to sell. Standard were wind-up windows, radio, and heater. Though this seems rather basic by today's standards, some sports cars back then had plastic flaps instead of windows on the doors, few had radios, and others didn't even have heaters! Yet even though it was a good value for the money, the Fairlady 1500 still wasn't the performance equal of most English and Italian sports cars.

But Nissan wasted little time in making it so. Power was increased for 1963 by using two carburetors instead of only one. The next year, engine size was increased to 1.6 liters, bringing horsepower up to 96. The car was then called the CSP311, and gained front disc brakes along with the added power. Smoother, quieter, and faster (top speed was now 100 mph), the CSP311 sold like hotcakes, especially in the U.S. A smoother running engine was used in 1965, and the name changed to SP311. The car was also an inch shorter, a half-inch narrower, and about two inches higher. Sold in the U.S. as the Datsun 1600, it looked like the cars shown here.

Even more power was added in 1967. A new 2.0-liter, overhead-cam engine with 135 horsepower was used with a 5-speed gearbox, and the car was now called the Datsun 2000. Weighing little more than the 1600, it could reach an easy 110 mph. (There was also a limited-production 145-horsepower racing version that could do over 125 mph.) Finally, Datsun had a full-blooded sports car.

Today, we recognize these little roadsters not only as a big step towards the famous Datsun 240Z that followed, but also as great sports cars in their own right. All things considered, these simple sporting Datsuns were a big success, which is one reason you still see them running around today. Like most Japanese cars of the Sixties, they weren't original in design, but they were a good value, built to last, and just plain fun. Perhaps things haven't changed so much after all.

The Datsun 1600 roadster sold well, especially in the U.S.

SPECIFICATIONS

Engine type	OHV inline-4 and SOHC inline-4
Displacement	90.8 cid/1488 cc to 121 cid/ 1982 cc
Horsepower	71 bhp @ 5000 rpm to 135 bhp @ 6000 rpm
Transmission	4-speed manual (1500/1600), 5-speed manual (2000)
Suspension	independent front/live rear axle
Brakes	front/rear drums (1500), front discs/rear drums (1600/2000)
Wheelbase (in.)	89.9
Weight (lbs)	2030-2110
Top speed (mph)	95-127
0-60 mph (sec)	10.2-15.5

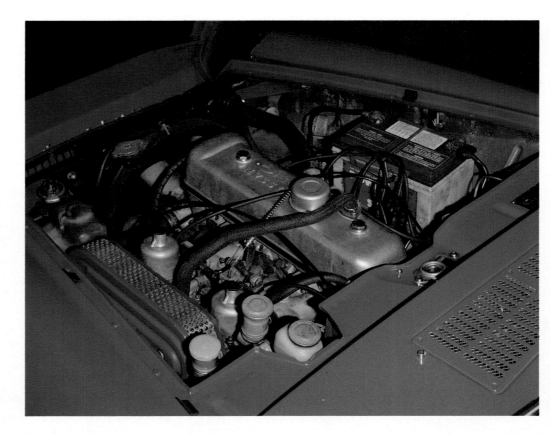

The Datsun 2000 roadster (1969 model shown here) featured an overhead-cam 2.0-liter engine and a 5-speed manual transmission; earlier 1600 models used an overhead-valve 1.6-liter and 4-speed manual. Top speed on the 2000 was 110 mph.

1970-1978 DATSUN 240Z/260Z/280Z

Having grown in both the number of models offered and the number of cars sold during the 1960s, Nissan looked to new ideas in the Seventies. It came out with a small, front-wheel-drive economy car that was sold in the U.S. as the F-10. Though it wouldn't win any prizes for its looks, the F-10 showed that the company could build a car that would appeal to a lot of people. But it was the 240Z that showed what this Japanese company could really do, helping Nissan to become what we now call a "world-class" automaker.

When the 240Z (called the Fairlady Z in Japan) was brought to the U.S. in 1970, it was a big hit. A far cry from the "boxy" 2000 roadster it replaced, the Z-car was a fastback coupe blessed with smooth, flowing lines, more than enough power, and a price that made it a bargain.

Designed at least in part by Count Albrecht Goertz, the 240Z was one of those cars that looks fast standing still.

The long hood, sweeping roofline, headlights deeply scooped into the front fenders, and rounded but angular shape just screamed "speed." It also reminded many people of the Jaguar E-Type—in performance as well as looks—which cost far more than the Z-car's $3526 list price.

The car's long nose was dictated partly by the engine, a 2.4-liter single-overhead-cam inline six-cylinder. With twin carburetors, it produced a healthy 151 horsepower in U.S. trim. The chassis was also impressive, with independent front and rear suspension, rack-and-pinion steering, and front disc brakes.

Sports cars of the day were often rather short on interior comfort, but the 240Z set a new standard for this price class. Full instrumentation, wall-to-wall carpeting, reclining bucket seats, radio, and a decent climate control system were all standard equipment. From the start, even air conditioning and automatic transmission

were optional, items most other sports cars didn't offer at any price.

Of course, none of this would have mattered had performance not matched the styling, but the 240Z delivered. Many raved about the 125-mph top speed, nimble handling, secure road-holding, and comfortable ride. And as time would tell, it would also offer good reliability—something that sports cars were not known for. In fact, a major reason for the 240Z's instant success was that it simply offered more than almost any other sports car of the day. The fact that it was not a convertible didn't seem to matter, and Nissan soon found it couldn't build Zs fast enough.

Demand would remain mostly strong through the end of this design in 1978.

The Datsun Z-car established Nissan Motor Corporation as a world-class automaker. Shown here is a 1976 280Z.

The original 240Z continued into 1973, when the engine was enlarged to 2.6 liters. The car then became the 260Z. Although it had a bigger engine, it was not as fast as the original. U.S. regulations were the cause. Emissions standards cut the horsepower of most engines back then, and the 5-mph bumper law forced the addition of bigger bumpers that added unwanted weight.

The 260 also marked the start of a trend to change the sporty Z into what is called a Grand Touring or GT car. GTs are usually heavier and more comfortable than sports cars, but they tend to be less fun as well. As if to signal the start of this trend, Nissan introduced a longer version of the 260Z that had a pair of tiny "+2" rear seats. These were large enough for children—but just barely.

Displacement rose to 2.8 liters in 1975, and the car became known as the 280Z. With 150 horsepower under the hood, the larger engine made the car almost as fast as the original 240 model. This was largely due to the use of fuel injection instead of carburetors.

After eight years and more than 540,000 units, the original Z-car came to an end in late 1978. More than any other, this was the car that proved Nissan could build not just transportation, but interesting, even exciting cars.

SPECIFICATIONS

Engine type	SOHC inline-6
Displacement	146 cid/2393 cc to 168 cid/ 2753 cc
Horsepower	139 @ 5200 rpm to 151 @ 5600 rpm
Transmission	5-speed manual or 3-speed automatic
Suspension	all independent
Brakes	front discs/ rear drums
Wheelbase (in.)	90.7 (2-seater), 102.6 (2+2)
Weight (lbs)	2300-2800
Top speed (mph)	115-125
0-60 mph (sec)	8.0-10.0

With exotic styling and a relatively low price, the Z-car was a big hit. This is a 1974 260Z.

1971-1990 DETOMASO PANTERA

Alejandro De Tomaso made his start as an automaker by building the low-production Mangusta (which means "mongoose" in Italian). It was a very low, sleek, mid-engine car that was designed and built in Italy, yet was powered by a 289-cubic-inch Ford V-8 engine. While the car was quite fast (it could do 155 mph), it didn't handle very well, and that made going fast a bit risky. It also had a cramped interior, almost no luggage space, and was hard to see out of. From 1967 through 1971, only about 400 Mangustas were built.

But during that time, De Tomaso decided to work on a bigger project: a mid-engine supercar for the American market. He wanted it to be a more practical design, and he certainly wanted to build more than 400 of them. Its name: Pantera.

Although the first Panteras were built on the Mangusta chassis, a new one was soon designed that fixed the handling problems. Both cars were about the same size, and De Tomaso kept the mid-engine layout. However, the Pantera body had sharp angles where the Mangusta had curves, and though still somewhat small inside, the Pantera was roomier and more practical.

Also carried over was the use of a Ford engine, but this time it was a 5.7-liter (351-cubic-inch) "Cleveland" V-8. Horsepower was rated at 310 for U.S. cars and 330 for European models. A 5-speed manual was the only transmission offered.

All in all, the Pantera was quite a car, and the people at Ford took notice. Chevrolet had long been bragging that the Corvette was "America's only sports car," and Ford saw the Pantera as a chance to compete with Chevy in that market. It was soon decided that the Pantera would be sold in the U.S. through Lincoln-Mercury dealerships, and Ford at last had a sports car.

The Pantera made quite a hit when it reached the U.S. for model year 1971. The reason was price. At around $10,000, it offered all the style of a Ferrari or Maserati for far less money. It also had a simple, well-known American engine that could be serviced almost anywhere. It even came with Ford's normal new-car warranty.

The Pantera offered all the style and excitement of a mid-engine Ferrari or Maserati for a fraction of the cost. It was powered by a strong, reliable 351-cubic-inch Ford "Cleveland" small-block V-8.

A good thing, too, because the Pantera was something less than a dream come true. Problems with engine overheating and high interior temperatures cropped up early, and performance wasn't all it should have been. Due to U.S. emission (smog) controls, horsepower had dropped to 250 by 1973.

The 5-mph bumper standards that also showed up about that time caused more problems. A black rubber nose guard was added in 1973, and bigger back bumpers were in place by 1974. Furthermore, tougher '75 standards would have required a major redesign, including a new engine. Ford decided it would be too costly to update the car, so it quit importing the Pantera after 1974.

Lincoln-Mercury says it sold 6091 Panteras in four years, but this figure might be high. In fact, some sources list the 1971-74 total as only 5629 units.

While it may sound as though this is the end to the Pantera story, it is not. The car continued to be sold in Europe (it proved especially popular in Germany), and is still in production at this writing. It's seen little change since 1974 apart from a switch to Australian-made Ford engines. A model called the GT5 is currently being built, which has add-on front spoiler, rear wing, and fender flares. The basic car, however, is the same one first offered by Ford almost 20 years ago.

Furthermore, Panteras started being imported to the U.S. again in 1981. This time, however, it is through a private company rather than through Ford. And although only about 50 cars are imported per year, you can once again buy a brand-new Pantera, this time with 300 to 350 horsepower. If that's not good news, we don't know what is.

Ford imported the Pantera through 1974, but didn't bring in later models because of the expense of meeting government standards. Pantera is still in production, and a private company sells about 50 per year in the U.S.

SPECIFICATIONS

Engine type	Ford OHV V-8
Displacement	351 cid/5763 cc
Horsepower	250-350 @ 5400-6000 rpm
Transmission	ZF 5-speed manual transaxle
Suspension	all independent
Brakes	front/rear discs
Wheelbase (in.)	99.0
Weight (lbs)	3100-3300
Top speed (mph)	140-160
0-60 mph (sec)	5.2-7.5

1968-1974 FERRARI 365 GTB/4 "DAYTONA" & 365 GTS/4 "DAYTONA SPIDER"

Among Ferrari's vast stable of magnificent cars, the 365 GTB/4, commonly known as the "Daytona," has to rank as one of the best. It's certainly one of the finest "street" Ferraris ever made. First shown at the 1968 Paris auto show, it was not only the most expensive roadgoing Ferrari, but also the fastest. *Road & Track* magazine verified the factory's claimed 174-mph top speed and ran the standing quarter-mile in a blistering 13.8 seconds. What Ferrari had here was nothing less than a "muscle car" Italian-style.

And what muscle. The Daytona carried a DOHC V-12 engine that was small by American standards—only 268 cubic inches. But its six carburetors helped the engine make a strong 352 horsepower at a screaming 7500 rpm.

While most cars have the transmission mounted directly behind the engine, the Daytona had a 5-speed that was part of the differential assembly mounted between (and driving) the rear wheels. When the

transmission and differential are combined into one unit, it is known as a transaxle. The main reason for using this type of design is to spread the weight of the car more evenly between the front and rear wheels. This gives the car better balance, which in turn gives it better handling and braking performance—nice to have when your top speed is over 170 mph.

Although it is hard to imagine, some Ferrari fans were not altogether pleased at first with the Daytona's styling. Now, however, there is little argument that this is one of the most beautiful Ferraris ever made. In fact, many Daytona styling elements have since shown up on a number of lesser cars (including a few replicas like the Corvette-based car on TV's *Miami Vice*). One design feature that originally graced the front end was a full-width plastic headlight cover. Unfortunately, American vehicle codes didn't allow such things, so hidden headlamps were used on U.S.-bound cars. Two years later, all Daytonas had them.

By the way, the Daytona name was

given to this car by the motoring press, not by Ferrari. It was nicknamed after the Daytona 500, a race held yearly in Daytona, Florida. But it stuck anyway, even though the factory referred to the cars as 365 GTB/4 (coupe), and 365 GTS/4 (roadster).

The Daytona feels heavy behind the wheel—and it is, especially for a two-seater. Although it has aluminum doors, hood, and trunklid, it tips the scales at nearly 3600 pounds—almost as much as a '68 Chevy Impala. But the weight seems to have little effect on handling, which is excellent. It also doesn't seem to have hurt performance, as the 0-60 mph and top speed figures prove.

Ferrari made few changes to the Daytona during its four short years other than the headlamp cover and the addition of a convertible model, called

The Daytona's brutish styling was controversial in its day, but the car is now widely recognized as one of the most beautiful Ferraris ever.

the "spider." Of the more than 1300 Daytonas built, only 127 were spiders.

Low production and high appeal explain why Daytonas are worth many times their original $20,000 price today. Convertibles generally command bigger bucks than coupes—sometimes almost twice as much—which explains why several shops now specialize in Daytona spider conversions. While some are done for owners who simply want a convertible and really want it to be a Daytona, we suspect most are done in an attempt to increase the car's value. If this keeps up, coupes could be in shorter supply one day and therefore, ironically enough, worth more than spiders, either converted or original.

A few Daytona coupes raced with success, some with lighter, all-aluminum bodywork and engines tweaked to 405 horsepower. They were formidable track performers, but brakes were a weakness of all Daytonas. Even race-equipped cars tipped the scales near 3600 pounds (bigger wheels and tires and the increased load of larger fuel tanks offset weight savings in bodywork and some mechanical pieces) and the brakes just weren't up to the car's 200-mph top speed.

The Daytona's front-engine design raised a few eyebrows in the late Sixties, mainly because other exotic cars—as well as Ferrari's own racing cars—were of mid-engine design. And as it turns out, this would be the last two-seat Ferrari with a front-mounted engine. The Daytona marked the end of an era, and for that reason alone, it will never be forgotten.

SPECIFICATIONS

Engine type	DOHC V-12
Displacement	268 cid/4390 cc
Horsepower	352 @ 7500 rpm
Transmission	5-speed manual (rear transaxle)
Suspension	all independent
Brakes	front/rear discs
Wheelbase (in.)	94.5
Weight (lbs)	3600
Top speed (mph)	170+
0-60 mph (sec)	5.9

Daytona "spiders," or convertibles, are so highly prized by collectors that they sometimes sell for twice as much as the coupes. Under that long hood is a potent double-overhead-cam V-12.

1975-1987 FERRARI 308/308i GTB/GTS & 328 GTB/GTS

Ferrari is best known for its legendary high-buck, low-production exotics, but it's important to remember that the company also makes some cars in significantly larger numbers. A couple of models have seen more than 4000 copies. By comparison, only 1500 Daytonas (both coupe and spider) were built, and most Ferraris are far more scarce than that. In fact, many are so rare that fewer than 100 exist in the world.

One of the first "mass-produced" cars was the Dino 246 GT coupe and 246 GTS spider (convertible). Strangely, neither carried the Ferrari name. The most likely reason is that the engine was a V-6 made by Fiat, whereas the "real" Ferraris of the day all sported V-12s. Nevertheless, the Dino was quite quick (0-60 mph in 8 seconds flat) and had a top speed of 140 mph. In its five years of production (1969-1973) about 4000 rolled off the

line. Though not officially a Ferrari, it was designed by Ferrari engineers, and the body was built by a regular Ferrari supplier.

Following the 246 was the Dino 308 GT4. Though fitted with a Ferrari-built, double-overhead-cam V-8 engine, it too lacked a Ferrari nameplate—but not Ferrari performance. Zero to 60 mph took just 6.4 seconds, and top speed was over 150 mph. Where the 246 was a swoopy, mid-engine two-

seater, the 308 GT4 was an angular, mid-engine 2+2. It carried on through the 1979 model year.

Ferrari traditionally previewed his new cars at Europe's fall auto shows. The Frankfurt, West Germany show came first (usually held the last two weeks of September, but only in odd-numbered years), followed by Paris, France (first two weeks of October), London, England (last half of that month), and Turin, Italy (first

half of November). Because of this yearly schedule, most Ferraris were introduced at Paris, and that's where the 308 GTB was first shown in 1975.

As on the 308 GT4, the model number (308) meant that the car was equipped with a 3.0-liter eight-cylinder engine—the same one, in fact, as was found in the Dino. For some reason, however, the 308 GTB was officially blessed with the Ferrari name.

This double-overhead-cam V-8

started out with four carburetors producing 205 horsepower. However, the two-seat GTB actually weighed a little more than the 2+2 GT4, so acceleration was just a bit slower.

In the styling department, however, it was no contest. The GTB looked more like an update to the original Dino, bringing back that car's flowing curves. Design features included a wide eggcrate grille riding below the bumper, hidden headlamps, bulging front and rear fenders, smooth fast-back roofline, and a square-cut rear end that housed four large round tail-lamps. Of particular interest were the long, triangular-shaped scoops that ran from the middle of the doors into the rear fenders—a styling element that would appear on several future Ferraris. At first, bodies for the GTB were made of fiberglass, but were soon switched over to steel, which was the usual Ferrari building material. In all, the 308 GTB was thoroughly modern yet not at all faddish. Thankfully, this basic shape hasn't changed much since.

Ferrari fans asked for an open (spider) version of the 308 GTB, and in 1977, they got it. Introduced at the Frankfurt show as the 308 GTS, the roof section over the cockpit could be removed and stored behind the seats. Known as a "Targa top," it is not a full-fledged convertible, since the rear half of the roof remains in place. However, it is less expensive to build because it requires only minor changes to the basic structure.

Meanwhile, Ferrari had introduced a 208 model (2.0 liters) for the Italian market, where taxes on cars with engines larger than 2.0 liters were very high. The 308 was mainly for export.

Mechanical improvements to the 308 GTB came slowly but surely. Fuel injection replaced the four carburetors in 1981, mostly to meet ever-tightening emissions regulations, and an "i" (for "injection") was added to the model names. Even better, 1982 brought a new V-8 with four valves per cylinder (32 in all), raising output to 230 horsepower. At the same time, a few minor detail changes were made,

including the addition of a small spoiler to the back edge of the roof, and bumpers that were changed from black to body color.

Bringing the story up to date are the 328 GTB/GTS, which came out in 1985. The new number reflects a displacement increase for the V-8 engine, from 3.0 liters to 3.2 liters. Horsepower likewise increased, from 230 to 260.

An instant success with the public and the automotive press alike, these Ferraris are delightful to drive and beautiful to look at. No wonder this series has become the most popular in Ferrari history. The 308/328 are great for town cruising or weekend jaunts, but aren't as good for long trips due to their small luggage space. Take one on a winding road, however, and its excellent power, handling and brakes can all be used—and enjoyed—as Ferrari intended.

SPECIFICATIONS

Engine type	DOHC V-8
Displacement	179 cid/2927 cc to 194.4 cid/ 3185 cc
Horsepower	205 @ 6600 rpm to 260 @ 7000 rpm
Transmission	5-speed manual (rear transaxle)
Suspension	all independent
Brakes	front/rear discs
Wheelbase (in.)	92.1 (308s), 92.5 (328)
Weight (lbs)	3085-3350
Top speed (mph)	130-149
0-60 mph (sec)	6.0-9.5

The 308/328 was never available as a full convertible, but GTS models (upper photo) had a removable roof panel that could be stored behind the seats. All 308/328s were two-seaters.

1985-1987 FERRARI TESTAROSSA

There are cars, and then there are supercars. In late 1984, Ferrari unveiled the Testarossa (which means "redhead" in Italian), named after one of its late-Fifties sports/racing cars. It went into production the following year as the first Ferrari to be designed with American safety and emissions standards in mind.

Unlike most previous roadgoing Ferraris, its body was made of lightweight aluminum except for a steel roof and doors. Even so, the Testarossa weighed in at nearly 3700 pounds—rather heavy for a "sports car."

Perhaps the most striking design feature was a set of long ribs or slats on each side. These covered two radiators, one per side, mounted just behind the passenger compartment. Tests indicated the slats (sometimes called "egg slicers") were needed in order to properly direct air into the radiators. They were also needed because some countries require body openings of this size to be covered with some sort of grillework. Placing the radiators in the back (rather than behind the grill) kept the interior cooler and also opened up more luggage space in the front.

The Testarossa engine was an unusual "flat-12" design, sometimes called a "boxer." It gets its name from the fact that it has two rows of pistons laid flat on their sides. The bottoms of the pistons in one row face the bottom of those in the other row, with the crankshaft in between. When the engine is running, the pistons move toward and away from each other, like two boxers fighting in a ring. The term was first used to describe the layout of early Volkswagen and Porsche engines, although those were rather small and had only four cylinders.

A simpler version of the Testarossa's flat-12 engine was used in an earlier Ferrari. It had two valves per cylinder, two carburetors, and produced 340 horsepower. The engine used in the Testarossa has four valves per cylinder, fuel injection, and is good for 380 horsepower. As if to justify the "Testarossa" name, the valve covers on each side of the engine are colored red—thereby making it a "redhead."

If you look at the car from the rear (which is the only view most other drivers ever get), you'll notice that the Testarossa is exceptionally wide. At almost 78 inches (that's six and-a-half feet), the car looks like it would take up two lanes. This width also gives the car a very wide turning circle (the space required for the car to make a U-turn), so it might not be the ride of choice when you have to find parking at a crowded mall.

The Testarossa is the first Ferrari designed specifically for the U.S.

But low-speed driving is not what this car was designed for, although it can lope along in rush hour traffic if need be. Speed is what the Testarossa is all about, and it delivers in spades. One ran the standing quarter-mile in 13.6 seconds at 105 mph in an early road test, while a later report (on a European delivery model) showed maximum velocity of no less than 181 mph. The 0-60-mph time was less thrilling perhaps—"only" 5.3 seconds—but for ground-level flying, the Testarossa is tough to beat.

As with some other Ferraris, not everyone is fond of the styling. But if imitation is indeed the sincerest form of flattery, the design must be considered a success. The side slats that are the Testarossa's trademark have now been widely copied, being found on several later production cars, as well as being used in various "add-on" body kits. As a matter of fact, we think the Testarossa will go down as one of the more distinctive Ferraris, if not the prettiest.

With a price tag of well over $100,000 at this writing, the Testarossa is not for everyone. But then, Ferrari never have been, and no doubt never will be. Like other Ferraris, the Testarossa demands respect on the road and a great deal of care off of it. Given these, however, the Testarossa will provide the ultimate thrill to even the most demanding drivers. The mighty Testarossa carries on the Ferrari legend, and will one day take its place in automotive history.

SPECIFICATIONS

Engine type	DOHC flat-12
Displacement	302 cid/4942 cc
Horsepower	380 @ 5750 rpm
Transmission	5-speed manual
Suspension	all independent
Brakes	front/rear discs
Wheelbase (in.)	100.4
Weight (lbs)	3660
Top speed (mph)	180
0-60 mph (sec)	5.3

Wild Testarossa styling features include bodyside ribs that cover cooling ducts. The 4.9-liter flat-12 engine propels the Testarossa to a top speed of 180 mph. "Testarossa" means "redhead" in Italian; note the red cylinder-head covers.

1972-1989 FIAT/BERTONE X1/9

Fiat's X1/9 wasn't the first mid-engine production sports car, but it has remained in production longer than any other we can think of. Announced in 1972, it was stylish, full of character, and thoughtfully equipped. It was also a remarkable value for the money.

It wasn't Fiat's first low-priced sports car, either. The giant Italian automaker had enjoyed good success in the Sixties with coupe and spider (convertible) versions of its little rear-engine 850 sedan, though these were sporty economy models, not genuine sports cars.

Bertone (an Italian automotive design firm) had supplied bodies for the 850 spider, and intended to provide the X1/9 (Fiat's internal project code) as a replacement for it. At first the idea was for Bertone to build the new mid-engine car from Fiat-supplied components. But Fiat soon realized the design as quite practical, and that it could be built "in-house."

The X1/9 followed the Lotus Europa and VW-Porsche 914 in being a two-seat sports car that had its own special body and chassis, but used mechanical pieces (engine, transmission, and such) borrowed from a regular sedan. In this case, the "regular sedan" was Fiat's little 128, introduced in 1969. Although the 128 had a front-mounted engine and front-wheel drive, it was a simple matter to move the engine/transmission package to the middle of the X1/9, and have it drive the rear wheels. Steering also came from the 128, as did the brakes, though the X1/9 was given disc brakes both front and rear.

Considering its small size, the X1/9 had a surprising amount of room. Much of this was due to its compact engine/transmission layout. Furthermore, its all-independent suspension not only gave a good ride and sticky handling, it was made up of only a few small parts and therefore took up little space.

Not only was there plenty of interior room for tall adults, there were even two trunks: one under the "hood" in the front of the car, and one in the normal place at the back of the car behind the engine. The fuel tank was between the passenger compartment and the engine, while the spare tire was mounted inside the car behind the passenger seat.

Bertone's wedge-shaped styling looked as good in '72 as it does today, and no doubt allowed for a lot of strength in the body design. A good thing, too, because besides having two doors, two trunk lids and a tilt-up engine cover, the X1/9 body also had a Targa roof. This meant there was a liftoff roof panel above the passenger compartment that could be stored in the front trunk. Since none of these panels could be counted on to provide stiffness to the body, the skeleton framework that was left had to be

quite strong indeed. In all, the X1/9 was a clever, well-thought-out package.

And surprisingly, a nicely balanced one, too. It is generally felt that the ideal design for a sports car is to have the car's weight split about evenly over the front and rear wheels (known as 50/50 weight distribution). But since the engine and transmission (both quite heavy) were mounted in the back of the X1/9, the car had most of its weight on the rear wheels. Even so, the steering and suspension system designs were so good that the X1/9

ended up being one of the better-handling cars around, and great fun to drive.

At first, the X1/9 wasn't as fast as it looked. The 1.3-liter SOHC four-cylinder engine that came from the 128 may have been okay for a lazy little sedan, but it just couldn't cut it as a sports car engine in the U.S. market. Part of this was due to the emissions controls required to make the little engine "smog legal." The rest can be blamed on the extra pounds added by federally required safety

gear (including 5-mph bumpers). Fiat made an attempt to boost performance for 1980 by swapping in a 1.5-liter engine, and replacing the original 4-speed transaxle with a 5-speed. This combination not only made the X1/9 a little faster, it also improved fuel economy. The following year, fuel injection was used in place of a carburetor, which resulted in another small gain in power.

These mechanical updates and some minor cosmetic and equipment revisions are pretty much the extent

of the changes made to the car over the years. However, Fiat decided to get out of the sports-car business in the early 1980s, so Bertone took over the manufacture and marketing of the X1/9. This led to various "special editions" in recent years, though the basic car remained the same. Later models may have worn the Bertone badge, but underneath, they're the same delightful little sports cars that hit these shores nearly 20 years ago.

SPECIFICATIONS

Engine type	SOHC inline-4
Displacement	78.7 cid/1290 cc to 91.4 cid/ 1498 cc
Horsepower	67 @ 5250 rpm to 85 @ 6000 rpm
Transmission	4-speed manual (1972-79), 5-speed manual (1980-87)
Suspension	all independent
Brakes	front/rear discs
Wheelbase (in.)	86.7
Weight (lbs)	2150-2250
Top speed (mph)	99-105+
0-60 mph (sec)	11.0-12.5

Bertone's styling for the X1/9 was always pretty, but later models suffered from bumpers that looked tacked on. Fiat left the U.S. market in the early Eighties, but Bertone took over U.S. distribution.

1971-1975 JAGUAR E-TYPE SERIES III V-12

Shortly after the end of the Second World War, Jaguar introduced a remarkable sports car called the XK120. It carried the world's first high-volume DOHC six-cylinder engine, which was assigned the name XK-series. This advanced engine was wrapped within a rounded, "streamlined" body, and the combination was claimed to be good for a 120-mph top speed, which explains the name XK120. Further refinements to the basic design appeared in 1954 (XK140) and again in 1957 (XK150). Though each showed a slight increase in performance over the previous model, the number designations did not indicate top speed as with the XK120.

Far ahead of its time when first introduced in 1948, the XK-series was beginning to show its age by the late 1950s. Sales-wise, it was still popular, but Jaguar knew it was time for an all-new design.

The replacement arrived in March of 1961, and though many people were sad to see the XK150 go, the new car put to rest any complaints. That first E-Type Jaguar was nothing

less than a sensation. Long, low, and curvy, it was available as a roadster (convertible) or fastback coupe. Underneath the hood (which seemed to make up half the length of the car) was the same smooth, powerful DOHC inline 6-cylinder engine found in the later XK150s, but now it could push either model to an honest 150 mph.

Thankfully, few changes were made during the E-Type's 11-year lifespan. In 1965, the engine grew from 3.8 to 4.2 liters, and the next year a longer 2+2 coupe with a small back seat joined the lineup. The Series II arrived for 1968. Styling suffered slightly due to U.S. safety standards, but included some refinements as well. By 1970, however, U.S. emissions standards were beginning to strangle the XKE's performance, and the engineers at Jaguar began looking for a cure. And cure it they did. In 1971, the Series III appeared with a huge V-12 engine that brought back the original performance—and then some.

Except for Ferrari and Lamborghini, no other automaker offered a production V-12 at the time. Large but beautifully

detailed, it featured all-aluminum construction (for lighter weight) and a single overhead camshaft for each bank of cylinders. With four carburetors, it produced 272 horsepower in European tune, and about 250 horsepower in U.S. trim. This 5.3-liter (326-cubic-inch) marvel was more powerful than the old six, but the XKE had now grown somewhat larger (and heavier) as well. To accommodate the bulkier, weightier engine, Jaguar discontinued the two-seat coupe and put the roadster on the same long wheelbase as the 2+2. The body and chassis were beefed up, wider wheels were mounted, and the all-disc brakes gained vented (instead of solid) rotors. Power steering was made standard.

Minor styling changes made what many thought was the best looking car in the world even better, despite the later addition of large, black rubber bumper guards required by U.S. 5-mph

This 1973 E-Type shows classic wire wheels. Black bumper guards were added for U.S. models.

bumper standards. A detachable factory hardtop arrived as a new roadster option, and instruments and interior detailing were cleaned up on both models.

The result was an E-Type that many judged superior to the 3.8-liter original of 1961—high praise indeed. And there was no question as to performance: At less than 7.5 seconds in the 0-60-mph test, the Series III offered acceleration in the same league as Ferrari and Lamborghini—and for far less money. The base price was around $8000 in 1972, making this the least expensive 12-cylinder sports car in the world.

For all its good points, however, the Series III had some flaws. Despite its large outside dimensions, interior room was tight. The beautiful bodywork was easily damaged, and the car continued to have electrical problems that had seemingly been passed down from generation to generation.

Fast and beautiful as it was, the Series III was doomed by the 1973-74 oil embargo that raised the price of gasoline. It was also hurt by the growing trend towards more "luxurious" sports cars. Jaguar replaced the XKE with the four-seat XJS in 1975, but to many, the new car would never have quite the same appeal.

However clumsy it may have seemed next to earlier E-Types, the Series III was widely loved, and many still hope for yet another V-12 sports car from Jaguar. But the XKE will be hard to top, for to some, it is nothing less than an automotive masterpiece.

SPECIFICATIONS

Engine type	SOHC V-12
Displacement	326 cid/5343 cc
Horsepower	250 @ 6000 rpm to 272 @ 5850 rpm
Transmission	4-speed manual or 3-speed automatic
Suspension	all independent
Brakes	front/rear discs
Wheelbase (in.)	104.7
Weight (lbs)	3230-3450
Top speed (mph)	135-142
0-60 mph (sec)	7.0-7.4

Jaguar's E-Type offered styling and performance comparable to much more expensive cars. The aluminum 5.3-liter single-overhead-cam V-12 could push the E-Type to 142 mph.

1974-1990 LAMBORGHINI COUNTACH

In 1966, Lamborghini brought out what was then considered the ultimate supercar of its day, the Miura. Only Lamborghini's second attempt at building a car (the company mostly made farm tractors and small appliances), the mid-engine Miura looked like it belonged on a racetrack, not the street. It also drove like it belonged on a racetrack; 0-60 mph took just over six seconds, and top speed was something on the far side of 170 mph. Strangely enough, one of its strengths was also one of its weaknesses. The pointed nose and flowing body lines that looked so good at 70 mph caused the car to want to "take off" at 170 mph, so top speed was limited as much by driver nerve as by horsepower.

When it came time to bring out a new supercar, Lamborghini knew the Miura was going to be tough to top. So did many observers. But when a prototype of the new car was shown in 1971, there were not only sighs of relief but gasps of amazement: No one had *ever* seen anything like the Countach.

And it's doubtful we will again soon.

Few cars have ever been blessed with the same visual and dynamic impact as the Countach. Today, in fact, more than 15 years later, it still looks like something out of the distant future. Only recently has anything come along that is any faster.

The Countach (pronounced COON-tahsh) is often described as the ultimate automotive fantasy. Its double-overhead-cam V-12 engine started out making 375 horsepower; the latest models, with four valves per cylinder, make as much as 455 horsepower. Instead of the more common pressed-steel chassis, it had a complex frame made of steel tubing. In place of side-opening doors, the ones on the Countach swing up and forward. Where most mid-engine cars of this type mount the engine sideways (sometimes referred to as "east-west") in the chassis, the Countach's sits lengthwise (called "north-south"). Actually, better make that "south-north," for the gearbox is placed forward of the engine—in fact, it extends into the passenger compartment between the seats. While this

doesn't do much for interior space, it does allow for a short, direct shift linkage, which in turn makes for crisp, positive gear changing.

The angular, sharp-edged body was drawn by Bertone's Marcello Gandini, who had also designed several other Lamborghinis, including the Miura. Some of the styling elements may have come from Bertone's 1968 Alfa-based Carabo show car, but the Countach was more muscular and mean-looking. Later models became even more so with the addition of various scoops, flares, and spoilers, which made them the visual equal of a solid punch to the jaw.

Officially called the LP400 by the factory, only 23 examples were sold in the Countach's first year of production (1974). But those customers found they had a 175-mph car capable of 0-60 mph in less than seven seconds, while turning every head on the way. Handling, braking, and high-speed stability were all of race-car quality.

Four years into its life, the Countach was given an update. Now called the LP400S, it received modified suspension geometry, a front spoiler, superwide Pirelli P7 tires on broader "five-hole" wheels, and wider fender flares to cover them. Optional was a huge rear wing, which made the Countach look even more like a racer.

With U.S. emissions standards (as well as tougher standards in Europe) beginning to take their performance toll, Lamborghini raised displacement to 4.75 liters in 1982, and called it the LP5000. But horsepower was still "only" 375—not enough—so in March 1985, Lamborghini again made the engine larger and added heads with four valves per cylinder. Called the LP5000S Quattrovalvole (which means "four valve"), the revised Countach made a genuine 455 horsepower in European tune (about 420 horsepower in the U.S.). The Countach was again king of the top-speed hill—over 180 mph—though its title as "world's fastest car" was often challenged.

Due to tough U.S. safety and emissions standards, the Countach was not officially imported into the states from the mid-Seventies through

about 1982. Some, however, were slipped in during that time by private individuals. But this is no longer a problem, and things are looking up again at Lamborghini (especially since Chrysler bought the company in 1987). Besides, it was worth the wait. Compared to the LP400S, the latest U.S. LP5000S Quattrovalvole packs 420 horsepower (versus 325), does 0-60 mph in 5.2 seconds (5.7 before) and reaches 173 mph (versus 150). But in case you think this kind of performance comes cheap, think again. During that time, the price of a Countach went from "only" $52,000 in 1976 to about $120,000 now.

And what do you get for your money? A rocky ride, terrible outward vision, engine noise near that of a jet on takeoff, a driving position only Plastic Man could love, and controls only Arnold Schwarzenegger can operate. But oh, that body and, oh, that speed!

Even after 16 years, the Countach still stands out as probably the most exotic car of all time. Although challengers from the likes of Ferrari and Porsche are getting ever stronger, ever faster, the Countach remains on top of the supercar heap—on styling if not on speed. And if you think about that, it's really quite amazing.

Like the car itself.

The angular, sharp-edged styling of the Lamborghini Countach looks like something from the distant future. Seeing the Countach, it's hard to believe that the company was best known for making farm tractors and small appliances.

SPECIFICATIONS

Engine type	DOHC V-12
Displacement	239.8 cid/3929 cc to 315.3 cid/ 5167 cc
Horsepower	325 @ 7500 rpm to 455 @ 7000 rpm
Transmission	5-speed manual (in rear transaxle)
Suspension	all independent
Brakes	front/rear discs
Wheelbase (in.)	98.4
Weight (lbs)	2915-3285
Top speed (mph)	173-192
0-60 mph (sec)	4.9-6.8

Shown here is the most recent Countach, which is powered by a 5.3-liter, double-overhead-cam V-12 with four valves per cylinder. Top speed is 192 mph.

1966-1975 LOTUS EUROPA

Lotus's mid-engine racing cars earned worldwide fame before the company ever got around to building a mid-engine road car. Not that it hadn't wanted to. Colin Chapman, an early 1950s race-car designer who was founder and president of Lotus, just couldn't find the right parts. Mainly, the transaxle (transmission and drive axle combined in one unit) that was needed to allow the engine to be mounted in the middle of the car wasn't being produced by any of the major manufacturers at that time. And ever since Chapman began making passenger cars in 1957, he had always used drivetrains (engines and transmissions) from other companies. Besides, Lotus was already busy building the popular Elan, a front-engine, two-seat roadster. (The design of which, some say, Mazda used as a basis for its new Miata sports car).

Then, in 1965, the French carmaker Renault brought out the front-wheel-drive model 16 sedan, and Chapman had his transaxle. He arranged to buy modified drivetrains from Renault for a new mid-engine model to be called the Europa.

What Chapman bought was the 16's 4-speed, front-drive transaxle, and a "hopped-up," 78 horsepower version of its 1.5-liter overhead-valve four-cylinder engine. Like other roadgoing Lotuses, the Europa had a fiberglass body that was mounted to a steel backbone frame with all-independent coil-spring suspension.

Styling was neat, but rather strange. The low nose with exposed headlamps was fine, but the back end looked odd, with broad, high sail panels running back from the doors all the way to the rear of the car. It looked a little like a very short, very flat station wagon, which earned the Europa the nickname "breadvan." A high engine cover made the tall sail panels necessary, leaving only enough space for just a slit of a rear window. As you might guess, backing up was a bit of a trick. Bodies and chassis were at first bonded together, which helped make for a strong, stiff package. Unfortunately, it also made

The mid-engine Lotus Europa used a fiberglass body attached to a steel frame. Styling was odd, but handling was great.

it hard to repair accident damage.

The first Europas were delivered in early 1967, and were sold factory-built or in kit form (the buyer could assemble the car). Lightweight construction again paid off in surprising performance with great fuel economy. The short, wide body and mid-engine layout resulted in the kind of handling the world had come to expect of Lotus—all this plus the usual fine ride and a reasonable price.

But all was not well in Lotus-land. Performance disappointed many people, as did the cramped interior, fixed door windows, and odd styling. Some people complained about sloppy workmanship. The Series 2 Europa, announced in 1968, answered some of these problems. The body was bolted to the chassis instead of bonded (to make repairs easier), power windows were installed, and a bit more space was found for luggage (behind the engine) and around the pedals. For the U.S. market, a larger 1.6-liter, 88-horsepower engine made up for power-sapping emissions controls.

Despite these improvements, an even better Europa was yet to come. In October 1971, the Series 3 Twin-Cam appeared, with a 105-horsepower DOHC four-cylinder engine. Unlike earlier engines used in the Europas, this one was made by Ford of England, but was fitted with Lotus's special DOHC cylinder head. It was the same engine used in the larger, heavier Elan roadster. The Renault transaxle, however, was retained. Styling was altered by cutting down the rear sail panels, which made for slightly better rear vision. Sharper-looking alloy wheels replaced plain steel ones. In this form, the Europa was good for up to 120 mph flat out (versus the previous 110).

Late 1972 brought the even better Europa Special, with a 126-horsepower "Big-Valve" engine and a new 5-speed Renault transaxle. By this time, the lightweight Europa had become a very quick sports car. Top speed was now over 125 mph, and the 0-60-mph sprint took less than 8 seconds.

However, Lotus had been hard at work on a larger, more powerful mid-engine replacement. Though seemingly getting better every year, the Europa was dropped after the 1975 model run. But with its lightweight fiberglass body (early models tipped the scales at less than 1400 pounds), fantastic handling, and (at least in later years) lively acceleration, the Europa passed into history much loved for its performance, if not its styling.

SPECIFICATIONS

Engine type	Renault OHV inline-4 Ford/Lotus DOHC inline-4
Displacement	89.7 cid/1470 cc to 95.0 cid/ 1558 cc
Horsepower	78 @ 6000 rpm to 126 @ 5500 rpm
Transmission	Renault 4- or 5-speed manual
Suspension	all independent
Brakes	front discs/rear drums
Wheelbase (in.)	94.0
Weight (lbs)	1350-1550
Top speed (mph)	109-121
0-60 mph (sec)	7.7-10.7

Europa started life with a Renault 1.5-liter overhead-valve engine, but later models used a double-overhead-cam powerplant based on a Ford engine.

1986-1990 MAZDA RX-7

The original Mazda RX-7, introduced in 1978, took the automotive world by storm. Here was a quick, nimble, good-looking, affordable sports car in the tradition of the first Datsun 240Z. By this time, however, the Datsun had grown a little too soft and a little too fat, leaving the low end of the market open for Mazda's sports car.

One of the RX-7's greatest features was its smooth, powerful rotary engine. Though styling was clean and modern and the price was right, the rotary engine is what really set the car apart. This was quite a turnaround considering that Mazda's first rotary engines, back in the early '70s, had earned the engine a poor reputation. Despite being very powerful for their size, they drank too much fuel and didn't last very long; not exactly popular traits, especially during the first energy crisis of '73. But those first models were supposed to be economy cars, so people expected good fuel mileage, and were disappointed. The RX-7, on the other hand, was a sports car, so people expected good performance—and got it. As icing on the cake, Mazda had fixed the gas-guzzling and reliability problems, making the little engine an almost ideal powerplant. Yet surprisingly, the RX-7 was—and still is—the only car in the U.S. to offer a rotary engine.

Despite favorable reviews, however, early RX-7s were not perfect. The ride was a bit stiff, the cockpit was cramped for taller people, and cornering on bumpy or wet surfaces could get a bit tricky. This last fault was likely due to the fact that the Mazda had a solid rear axle rather than the superior and more common (at least in sports cars) independent rear suspension. Though the original RX-7 sold like hotcakes throughout its six-year model run, eventually it was time for an update.

The second-generation RX-7 came to the U.S. in 1986, sleeker, more stylish—and more powerful. The little rotary started out with 100 horsepower in '78, which was boosted to 135 horsepower in some models for 1984-85. The '86s got a slightly bigger engine with fuel injection that produced 146 horsepower. If that wasn't enough, a new turbocharged model was available that offered 182 horsepower. Unfortunately, weight had gone up as well. The base '86 weighed about 240 pounds more than the '85, and the Turbo added another 225 pounds to that, though size stayed about the same. Still, the base cars were faster and the Turbo was a real flyer. The Turbo wasn't available with automatic transmission, but non-turbos were: a new 4-speed overdrive unit, replacing the non-overdrive 3-speed used before.

Longer and sleeker than the original RX-7, the new model featured a larger engine and independent rear suspension. Shown here is a 1989 GXL.

The chassis offered further improvements. Rack-and-pinion steering provided a crisper feeling than the old recirculating-ball setup. Out back, the old live rear axle was replaced by a new independent suspension system, and rear disc brakes were fitted instead of drums.

The sports-car field had gained more players by this time, and had become highly competitive. It was difficult to design a car that didn't look at least a little like someone else's. And that was one of the few complaints about the new RX-7; it didn't have the unique look of the original car. The car still rode stiffly, but the interior offered more useful space.

Although response to the styling was lukewarm, the new RX-7s earned rave reviews. Most critics agreed that it was even better than the old one, saying that it "raises the standards for sports-car performance." All in all, it was a quick, nimble, good-looking sports car at a bargain price—just like the original.

As of this writing, the second-generation story is far from over. Further improvements are being added every year, new models with racing-style bodywork are being offered, and horsepower ratings continue to climb. But whatever happens in the future, the second-generation RX-7 will go down in automotive history as a great sports car. The original RX-7 may have been tough to follow, but in this case, success has bred success.

SPECIFICATIONS

Engine type	2-rotor Wankel
Displacement	80 cid/1308 cc
Horsepower	146 @ 6500 rpm to 200 @ 6500 rpm
Transmission	5-speed manual, 4-speed automatic
Suspension	all independent
Brakes	front disc/rear drum (rear discs on certain models)
Wheelbase (in.)	95.7
Weight (lbs)	2625-2850
Top speed (mph)	125-135+
0-60 mph (sec)	8.5-9.0

Though some people thought the second-generation RX-7 looked bland compared to the original, it remained an attractive, fun-to-drive car at an appealing price.

1962-1980 MGB AND MGB GT

When many people think of the term sports car, the MGB is the first one that pops to mind. This may partly be due to numbers. Though the roadster was far more popular than the GT hatchback coupe, together, over half a million were produced—far more than any other sports car we can think of.

The MGB evolved from a long line of two-seat roadsters, dating back to the MG TA that came out in 1936. Though the first model imported into the U.S. was the MG TC of 1945, it differed very little from the original TA. Both were short, narrow, and fragile-looking, with tall, thin radiator grills and separate fenders that swept back from the front wheels and looped over the rears. Compared to American cars of the day, they were old-fashioned (they didn't even have roll-up side windows), hard-riding, and slow. However, they were a blast to drive and completely different from anything else on the road. As such, they picked up a small but loyal following.

These T-series MGs changed little through 1955. The MG TD that came out in 1949 brought independent front suspension, while the TF, which was built from 1953-55, eventually added a larger engine with a whopping 63 horsepower. But by this time, the MGs badly needed an update.

It came in the form of the MGA. Virtually all-new from the ground up, the MGA had a modern, rounded look, and was built on a strong steel frame rather than the wood frame that supported the T-series. It also got a bigger engine with 72 horsepower, which raised top speed from about 80 mph to almost 100 mph. Though the roadster still lacked side windows and outside door handles, a coupe version soon appeared that carried both those features.

The MGA carried on until 1962 with few changes. A bigger, 80-horsepower engine arrived for '59, along with front disc brakes. Another small power increase came in 1961, making the MGA a true, 100-mph sports car.

An interesting variation of the MGA was introduced in 1958. It was equipped with a double-overhead-cam engine that made 108 horsepower and brought top speed to 113 mph. Unfortunately, the "Twin Cam," as it was known, cost 25 percent more than the standard MGA. Furthermore, engine problems soon cropped up, making the car unpopular with buyers. Only 2111 were built before MG quit making them in 1960.

Which brings us to the MGB. Announced in the fall of '62, the new model rode a three-inch-shorter wheelbase, but had more interior and luggage space. It was also equipped with a larger, more powerful engine, and even had roll-up side windows. Though the suspension dated back to the MG TD of ten years earlier, the car provided surefooted handling and a fairly smooth ride.

All in all, the MGB was stylish and (finally) quick enough to keep up with its sports-car competition. The price was right, too: around $2500 at introduction. Altogether, it was a winning combination. U.S. sales, which began at the end of '62, were strong. More than 23,000 MGBs were built in calendar 1963, a new yearly record that was promptly broken with 26,542 units in '64.

For some years, the MGB could do no wrong. It received minor running changes along the way, and a hatchback coupe model, called the MGB GT, was added in '65. Elegant yet practical, it could double as daily transportation for a small family. Two years later, a smoother-shifting transmission and stronger rear axle appeared, along with MG's first-ever automatic transmission option. The automatic wasn't popular, however, and only about 5000 MGBs were so equipped before it was discontinued in 1973.

Unfortunately, this would mark the high point of MGB development. Though European models carried on mostly unchanged, those shipped to the U.S. suffered badly from cheap solutions to the stricter safety and emissions standards in the Seventies. For instance, in order to meet U.S. headlight height regulations, the suspension was simply jacked up by

1.5 inches, which didn't do the handling any good. Ugly black energy-absorbing bumpers were tacked on front and rear, and engines were choked down to just 62 horsepower. And the neat little MGB GT coupe was dropped altogether.

With all this, late-model U.S. MGBs couldn't top 90 mph. Americans also missed out on a GT coupe that was fitted with a powerful V-8 engine, but offered only in England. No heavier than the standard MGB GT, the V-8 could hit 60 mph from rest in 7.7 seconds, versus 18.3 for the four-cylinder U.S. car. Still, only 2591 were built.

Age finally caught up with the MGB in 1980. It had been in production for 18 years without any major changes, and with sales in the U.S. market almost at a standstill, the company ran into money problems. The last MGB was built in October of that year, after which the factory was closed down. Special "farewell" models were offered in England, and the U.S. got a number of all-black roadsters as a going-away present. Sadly, these would be the last of what was once the best-known sports car in America, if not the world.

The MGB was much more modern than the MGA it replaced. Quick, stylish, and well priced, the MGB sold especially well in the U.S. The wooden steering-wheel rim and gearshift knob are classically British. Power was supplied by a 1.8-liter overhead-valve four-cylinder engine that gave a top speed as high as 103 mph.

SPECIFICATIONS

Engine type	OHV inline-4
Displacement	109.7 cid/1798 cc
Horsepower	62 @ 5400 rpm to 95 @ 5400 rpm
Transmission	4-speed manual with optional overdrive (standard U.S. from 1975), 3-speed automatic (1967-73)
Suspension	independent front/live rear axle
Brakes	front discs/rear drums
Wheelbase (in.)	91.0
Weight (lbs)	2030-2600 (roadster), 2190-2260 (GT)
Top speed (mph)	90-103
0-60 mph (sec)	12.2-18.3

Shown here is the last of the MGBs, a 1980
model with U.S. bumpers.

1984-1989 NISSAN 300ZX

To many sports-car lovers, the original 240s were the best of the Z-cars, and the line has gone downhill ever since. Certainly the 280ZX that came out in 1979 was a heavier, plusher vehicle, and many complained that it wasn't really a sports car anymore at all. Such items as power steering, cruise control, fancy radios, and power windows were made either standard or optional along the way, and some felt the Z was now more of a luxury liner.

Likewise, history probably won't be kind to the first-series 300ZX either. That's understandable when you consider that in concept, it is little more than an updated 280ZX, even though it is an all-new design.

When the 300ZX was introduced in 1984, Z-lovers and auto writers alike could hardly hide their disappointment. "The same—only more so," said one car magazine. "It all seems to add up to a change for the difference," said another. In dimensions, chassis design, even styling, the 300ZX was amazingly similar to the 280ZX.

Not that there weren't differences. One of the most important was what one writer termed the 300ZX's "heart of gold": a new single-overhead-cam 3.0-liter V-6 engine—smoother, quieter, and more powerful than the 280ZX's inline six. Styling was leaner, cleaner, and smoother, but many felt that it was a little boring. Others weren't too fond of the semi-hidden headlamps, feeling that such styling gimmicks had no place on a sports car.

Still, some changes were for the better. Detail improvements included wider wheels and tires, and a new 4-speed automatic transmission option with electronic control (replacing the previous 3-speed). Inside, there was a slightly roomier cockpit with even more luxury features than the already-plush 280ZX, but again, many felt the Z was sliding further and further away from its sports car origins.

The 300ZX continued with the same three models as the last of the 280ZXs: two-seat and 2+2 coupes and turbo-charged two-seater. The Turbo models came with electronically adjustable shock absorbers. A switch on the console allowed the driver to choose between Soft (for a more comfortable ride), Normal, or Firm (for better handling). As with Goldilocks, the middle setting seemed just right. Soft produced too much bounce and cornering roll, while Firm could jar your teeth loose over bumps.

As it turns out, refinement was one of the 300ZX's great strengths. We still fondly remember a short California trip, driving through the mountains in an '85 Turbo with T-tops. The car really came into its own on empty two-lane roads, powering through high-speed corners with great ease. Yet it rode smoothly and quietly, never annoying us with a rocky ride or loud engine noise.

For better or worse, the 300ZX was changed very little through the 1989 model year. The '85s were the first to offer T-tops as standard equipment, though solid-roof non-turbo models with lower prices came back for 1986. That year also brought fender flares, rocker skirts, body-color bumpers, new sports seats, and minor interior changes, along with big, 16-inch wheels for Turbo models. Styling was improved for '87 with a smoother nose, new wheels, and full-width taillamps.

Even with these year-to-year improvements, however, the 300ZX went on a steady sales slide until it was replaced for 1990 with a radically new design. The good news is that Nissan has returned to the kind of thinking that produced the first 240Z, having learned that playing it safe doesn't always improve sales. It also doesn't produce the kind of excitement and interest enjoyed by the original Z-car.

Now that the stunning new 300ZX is here, the old 300ZX probably won't be missed much, worthy though it is. But history may record it as a good example of how running in place isn't going to make you any headway in a competitive car market, and there must be some value in that.

The third-generation Z-car's styling seemed like a diluted version of the original Z. The T-tops were standard on this 1985 Turbo.

SPECIFICATIONS

Engine type	SOHC V-6
Displacement	181 cid/2960 cc
Horsepower	160 @ 5200 rpm to 205 @ 5200 rpm
Transmission	5-speed manual or 4-speed automatic
Suspension	all independent
Brakes	front/rear discs
Wheelbase (in.)	91.3 (2-seater), 99.2 (2+2)
Weight (lbs)	3050-3150
Top speed (mph)	125-130
0-60 mph (sec)	7.2-9.1

The 300ZX used a new single-overhead-cam V-6 instead of the older car's inline-6. Shock absorbers on the new 300ZX Turbo could be adjusted to three levels of firmness with the flick of a switch. Turbos were available as two-seaters only, but the non-turbo model offered a choice of two-seater or 2+2 with a small rear seat.

1984-1988 PONTIAC FIERO S/E & GT

Fiero means "proud" in Italian, and that's how Pontiac felt about its car of that name. Why? Because the Fiero was not only Detroit's first mid-engine car, but also America's only two-seat production car besides the Corvette.

Pontiac had been wanting to build a rival to Chevy's sports car for almost 20 years. Although it was designed at first as a "commuter car," Pontiac engineers had high hopes of one day making it a true competitor to the Corvette. After all, the basic design had all the right stuff: mid-mounted engine (like many high-priced European sports cars), "skeleton" frame, and lightweight plastic body panels. However, Pontiac's problem had always been that such a car would have to be sold in great enough numbers to make up for the expense of developing it. Since a high-performance car like the Corvette sells very few copies in a year, Pontiac's only choice was to start out with a racy economy car that would appeal to a great number of buyers.

And at first, anyway, it did. Though the engine and transmission were borrowed from the rather plain front-wheel-drive X-cars (like the Chevy Citation), the body looked anything but ordinary. As planned, it was a two-seat coupe with clean, angular styling. The only engine available at first was a 2.5-liter four-cylinder, along with either a 4-speed manual transmission or 3-speed automatic.

Unusual for a GM project, Fiero engineering development was assigned to an outside firm, Entech of Detroit. Basic styling came from Advanced Design III, and was then finalized at Pontiac's studios. Corporate cash-flow problems almost killed the project several times in 1980-82, but those working on the car fought hard to save it. They argued that the Fiero not only made financial sense, but was necessary to inject new life into a Pontiac image that had become boring and stale.

The result was a "corporate kit car," one that borrowed parts from other cars already being made by the same company. The engine, transmission, and front suspension (which would now be the rear suspension on the Fiero) was picked off of the X-car assembly line in one unit and mounted behind the cockpit. Front suspension,

steering, and brakes came from the lowly Chevy Chevette. This kind of "parts-swapping" allowed the car to get into production quicker and at less cost.

What was all new, however, was the space-frame chassis structure to which various plastic (not fiberglass) body panels were attached. This type of construction was revolutionary, at least for General Motors. For one thing, it allowed for easy, inexpensive styling changes, since only new plastic body panels needed to be stamped out to give the car a whole new look. In the interest of quality control, only four color choices would be offered at any one time.

Arriving in base and sportier S/E trim, Fiero received wide and mostly favorable press coverage. "Buff books" liked the handsome styling and overall design, but wished for a quieter, lighter car with more power, a 5-speed gearbox, smoother ride, and less twitchy cornering.

Pontiac responded. A Fiero was named as the Pace Car for the 1984 Indy 500, and it was equipped with a ground-hugging nose that later showed up on production models. This returned for 1985 on a new GT model powered by Chevy's fuel-injected V-6 engine (also from the X-cars) with 52 percent more power than the base four-cylinder engine. Standard rear

spoiler, "ground-effects" bodyside extensions, upgraded suspension, and a mellow exhaust system enhanced the new GT's mini-muscle-car feel.

This same package, though with the four-cylinder engine, became the 1986 S/E model. It was followed at mid-season by a new GT carrying revised rear fenders and fastback roofline. The promised 5-speed transmission finally arrived late in the model year. Changes for 1987 were limited to a larger fuel tank and minor trim revisions.

The sporty Fiero became even more so for 1988 as it finally got its own suspension. The new pieces gave the car tighter handling and made the car a lot more fun to drive. However, steering remained manual—and rather difficult at low speeds—though Pontiac hinted that power steering was just around the corner.

By this time, the Fiero had grown from its original base-model "commuter

car," into a genuine sports machine that was downright exciting with the right options. The 1988 version was the best Fiero ever, but sadly, it would also be as good as the Fiero would ever get. Although it had finally started to become the sports car Pontiac engineers had dreamed of, Fiero sales had gone down every year, despite the addition of new models. Pontiac finally discontinued the Fiero in the spring of 1988—a real shame, for it had become a great looking, great performing car. Furthermore, it carried the most innovative engineering seen from Detroit in years. One day, maybe they'll be more appreciated.

The Fiero GT offered exciting looks and good performance. Shown here is the 1988 model GT with its fastback roofline, rear spoiler, and bodyside extensions. Powering the GT was a 2.8-liter overhead-valve V-6.

SPECIFICATIONS

Engine type	OHV V-6
Displacement	173 cid/2837 cc
Horsepower	135 @ 4400 rpm to 140 @ 5200 rpm
Transmission	4- and 5-speed manuals or 3-speed automatic
Suspension	all independent
Brakes	front/rear discs
Wheelbase (in.)	93.4
Weight (lbs)	2750-2860
Top speed (mph)	105-120
0-60 mph (sec)	7.7-8.5

Shown below is the first Fiero GT, a 1985 model. At right is a 1988 GT. For 1988, Pontiac stopped using off-the-shelf suspensions from other GM cars, and handling was greatly improved. However, declining sales forced Pontiac to stop making the Fiero in the spring of 1988.

1978-1989 PORSCHE 911

Porsche's first sports car, the 356, was born in the late 1940s. Sometimes referred to as the "bathtub" Porsche (because it was shaped like an upside-down bathtub), it was powered by a modified Volkswagen flat-4 engine. With only minor revisions (larger, more powerful engines and the addition of a fastback coupe being the most notable), the 356 carried on for more than 15 years.

A replacement finally arrived in the mid-1960s. Called the 911, it looked like a sleeker version of the 356 fastback coupe. Power came from a single-overhead-cam flat-6 engine of Porsche's own design. Another version, called the 912, had the new body, but carried the old flat-4 engine.

The early 356 was a cute, fun little car, and it made a lot of friends in the U.S. The 911 had a more serious look to it, with power to match. While the faster versions of the 356 could sprint from 0-60 mph in about 10 seconds, some early 911s could do it in less than 7 seconds, with a top speed of 140 mph. And they would soon get even faster.

For instance, the incredible turbo-charged 911s that first came out in 1975 (and are still with us today) can do the 0-60-mph dash in about 5 seconds (some in a little less) and top out at over 150 mph.

But the focus here is on the "standard" 911s, which first arrived in this form in 1978, and remain in production as of this writing. Surprisingly, they look only slightly different from those first 911s that appeared in the mid-Sixties, and most of the changes are merely due to the addition of the required 5-mph bumpers.

When Porsche unveiled its '78s at the September 1977 Frankfurt auto show, there were only two 911s: a 3.3-liter Turbo and the new 3.0-liter, non-turbo 911SC. For 1977, 911s carried a 2.7-liter engine, and the displacement increase brought a power increase as well—from 157 to 172 horsepower. Actually, a special version of the 911, called the Carrera, had been available with the 3.0-liter engine before. Though horsepower was down slightly from that of the Carrera, a flatter, fuller torque curve made the SC somewhat easier to drive.

Except for Porsche's typical ongoing improvements and one major development that we'll get to shortly, the 911SC would continue in this form with little change through 1983. U.S. models became somewhat plusher in these years. Air conditioning, power windows, center console, and matte-black exterior trim were no-cost extras for 1980. Halogen headlamps and rear seatbelts were added for '81. The 1982s received standard headlight washers, leather front seats, and upgraded radio.

The first factory-built Porsche 911 convertible appeared in 1982.

But the most important 1982 change was shown at the Geneva show in March: the long-rumored 911SC cabriolet, the first true factory-built Porsche convertible since the last 356 model of 1965. For 1984, the SC became the 911 Carrera, reviving the famous model name used on and off since 1953. Another enlargement of the engine (to 3.2 liters) and a revised fuel-injection system boosted output to 200 horsepower. This marked the fifth such displacement increase since 1964.

Other 1984 changes included improvements to the braking system, a set of foglights built into the front spoiler, and an optional appearance package that made the Carrera look (and handle) like the mighty turbo version.

Few changes were made for 1985 and '86. But for 1987, horsepower went from 200 to 214, and modifications to the clutch and gearshift made shifting easier. Top speed was up to 149 mph and 0-60-mph acceleration down to 6.1 seconds.

A new Club Sport option for the coupe arrived in 1988. Intended for weekend racers, it trades such "luxury" features as air conditioning and sound insulation for stronger shock absorbers, sports seats, and a higher rpm limit.

And so it goes. The 911 celebrated its 25th anniversary in 1989, and we hope many more will follow, for it just keeps getting better and better. This is one car that is truly a legend in its own time.

SPECIFICATIONS

Engine type	SOHC flat six
Displacement	182.6 cid/2993 cc to 193 cid/ 3164 cc
Horsepower	172 @ 5500 rpm to 214 @ 5900 rpm
Transmission	5-speed manual
Suspension	all independent
Brakes	front/rear discs
Wheelbase (in.)	89.4
Weight (lbs)	2740-2750
Top speed (mph)	126-149
0-60 mph (sec)	6.1-6.7

Pictured here is the 1986 911 Carrera. Though styling has changed little in over 20 years, yearly improvements have made the 911 much faster and better handling. The familiar single-overhead-cam flat-6 now uses a sophisticated electronic fuel injection and engine management system.

1982-1990 PORSCHE 944/944 TURBO/944S

In September 1981, like so many times before, the Frankfurt auto show witnessed the public unveiling of a new Porsche: the 1982-model 944. Though based on the 924 that had been introduced in 1975, the 944 incorporated several small changes—and one big one.

The original 924 broke with tradition in that it not only had the first water-cooled engine Porsche had ever offered (all others were air-cooled),

but the engine was mounted in the front rather than in the rear. This brought howls of protest from loyal fans, because "Porsche" had always meant air-cooled, rear-engined sports cars, and it was one thing that set them apart from all the others. To this group of people, the 924 just didn't deserve to be called a Porsche.

Furthermore, the engine itself was also part of their complaint, for it was not actually a Porsche engine at all.

By that time, Porsche, Audi, and Volkswagen had joined together to form sort of a German General Motors. Since the 924 was originally planned to be a Volkswagen model that was designed by Porsche engineers, most of the mechanical pieces were already being used in various Volkswagen and Audi vehicles. This included the engine, suspension, brakes, and steering. However, it was decided the new car would wear a Porsche nameplate, and, as mentioned before, this caused quite a ruckus. But those who objected seemed to forget that most of the mechanical parts of the very first Porsche (the 356) also came from Volkswagen, and that didn't seem to do it any harm.

Another complaint was that the 924 just didn't look like a Porsche. This was largely due to the front-engine layout, of course, but as far as Porsche fans were concerned, it was just another strike against the "new kid on the block."

Another "unusual" feature of the 924 was its transmission. Actually, it was a transaxle, which means that the transmission and rear axle were combined into one unit. Therefore, the engine was in the front of the car, while the transmission was in the back. One advantage to using this design is that it helps to divide the total weight of the vehicle more evenly between the front and rear wheels. This results in better balance, which in turn tends to improve handling and braking. It was also a forecast of things to come, for this front-engine/rear-transaxle arrangement would soon be used in other new Porsche models.

One more thing. The 924 was the first Porsche ever offered with a fully automatic transmission—one more strike against it, at least according to "real" Porsche fans.

The 944 that came along in 1982 was largely based on the 924, but there were enough differences to warrant the new model name. It used the same body as the 924, except that it had slightly different nose and tail styling, along with "bulging" front and rear fenders to cover wider wheels and tires. But the real news was under the hood.

First of all, the engine was larger and more powerful, but more importantly, it was all Porsche. As on the 924, it was a single-overhead-cam inline four—water-cooled, of course—but this time it was based on the big V-8 engine

The first Porsche 944 convertible appeared for 1990. Engine size increased to 3.0 liters, with four valves per cylinder.

used in the company's expensive 928 sports car (which followed the 924 in having a front-engine/rear-transaxle layout). In fact, the 944's engine looked like the V-8 with one bank (four cylinders) cut off—which it was. Displacement was 2.5 liters versus the original 924's 2.0 liters.

Four-cylinder engines larger than 2.0 liters are usually rough runners, so Porsche added two rotating balance shafts to smooth it out. U.S. 944s offered 147 horsepower, enough to run 0-60 mph in a brisk 8.3 seconds, with a top speed of 130 mph.

Needless to say, the engine swap made all the difference, and the 944 was deemed a true Porsche by auto writers and fans alike. The new engine was not just smooth but also very strong and quiet—just what the 924 had needed. Sales figures confirmed the appeal of this winning package, which, with few changes, is still being built at the time of this writing.

The first big change was made for 1986, when a turbocharged model was added. As might be expected, this

engine delivered a healthy helping of extra power and torque, bringing the 0-60 mph time down to 6.1 seconds and boosting top speed to over 150 mph.

Turbo models looked a little different than the standard models, too. Wide cooling slots were added to the nose, along with a combination bumper/front spoiler. A larger rear spoiler and wider wheels and tires were also included. The wheels were a five-hole design borrowed from the big 928.

Another new member of the 944 family arrived in mid-'86: the 944S. It fell between the normal 944 and the Turbo model in terms of power, speed, and price. Power was increased over the standard engine by adding a 16-valve, double-overhead-cam cylinder head.

For 1987, anti-lock brakes arrived as options on the 944S and Turbo. Airbags for both driver and passenger were standard for the Turbo and optional for other models. The airbags were made standard on the 944S for '88, and power rose slightly on the base engine. For '89, engine size was increased to 2.7 liters on the 944 and

to 3.0 liters on the 944S.

A 944 convertible, first planned as a late '89, arrived for 1990. The turbo was dropped, and the 3.0-liter DOHC engine was made standard on the two remaining models, now called 944 S2.

These were turbulent years for Porsche. Rapid price increases and the arrival of less expensive, luxuriously equipped competitors from Japan battered the small carmaker, and sales slid alarmingly. Sadly, the 944 was being squeezed out of the class it virtually created.

Though never what one would call cheap, the 944 costs a lot less than the 911, yet delivers performance worthy of the Porsche name. As a true driver's car, it has long been used as the yardstick by which other cars of this type are measured, and that in itself is perhaps the greatest form of praise.

944 Turbo models featured distinctive styling touches, such as a special front bumper with cooling slots and a spoiler. Wider wheels and tires, along with a larger rear spoiler, were used.

SPECIFICATIONS

Engine type	SOHC/DOHC inline-4
Displacement	151 cid/2479 cc to 182 cid/2991 cc
Horsepower	147 @ 5800 rpm to 247 @ 6000 rpm
Transmission	5-speed manual
Suspension	all independent
Brakes	front/rear discs
Wheelbase (in.)	94.5
Weight (lbs)	2900-3060
Top speed (mph)	123-153
0-60 mph (sec)	6.1-9.0

1964-1967 SUNBEAM TIGER

The Sunbeam Tiger was yet another small European car fitted with a big American V-8 engine, but this one cost a lot less than most of the others. In 1962, Carroll Shelby had stuffed a Ford V-8 engine into the A.C. Ace—another British sports car—to make the A.C. Shelby-Cobra. Sunbeam did the same with its little Alpine, but this car was a lot more affordable—yet just as exciting. Called the Tiger, it had a lot in common with the A.C.—not surprising, since Shelby built the prototype around the same basic Ford V-8.

The four-cylinder Sunbeam Alpine had earned a fine reputation by the mid-Sixties, especially in the U.S. But everyone agreed it would be a lot better if it had a more powerful engine. Trouble was, Sunbeam didn't have one. So the company decided it would buy a V-8 engine from Ford, and got Shelby to work out the details.

The result was introduced at the New York Auto Show in April 1964 (the same month as Ford's trend-setting Mustang). At that time, Sunbeam was a part of the Rootes Group (much like Chevrolet is a part of GM) and because the Rootes factories were taken up with the Alpine and family-car production, Tiger assembly was farmed out to Jensen, a specialty manufacturer.

Visually, the Tiger was much like the Alpine except for different badges, wheel covers, and full-length bodyside chrome strips. This similarity partly explains limited Tiger sales, as American buyers seemed to want their neighbors to *know* they had something special. It also seemed a problem in England, where sales began during 1965.

Like the first Shelby-Cobra, the Tiger arrived with the 260-cubic-inch version of Ford's new-for-'62 V-8 engine, although in a much milder state of tune. Even so, its 164 horsepower was more than twice what the Alpine had. A 4-speed manual transmission and live (sometimes called "solid") rear axle also came from Ford.

The chassis was the same as the Alpine's, which was nothing special. But Shelby took the opportunity to change from recirculating-ball steering to rack-and-pinion (which gave a "tighter" steering feel), added stiffer springs and shocks, and changed the rear suspension to help it handle the additional power. Brakes remained front discs and rear drums.

As might be expected, the Tiger made a big hit with the automotive writers, who were impressed with the car's new-found power. The Tiger cut the Alpine's 0-60-mph time almost in half, and its top speed was some 18 mph higher. Handling, roadholding, and ride comfort all earned high marks, though the combination of skinny tires and powerful engine meant that it was too easy to spin the rear wheels on take-off. But this was easy to forgive considering the kind of performance offered, especially when combined with the practical basic package inherited from the Alpine. The Tiger may not have been as fast as the A.C. Shelby-Cobra, but it was far more civilized, better equipped, and much cheaper. In fact, at $3499, it was almost a steal.

Unfortunately, an unusual problem came up shortly after introduction. Chrysler Corporation (the American automaker) became part-owner of Rootes just as the Tiger was about to go on sale. Shortly afterward, Lord

Shown here is a Mark I Sunbeam Tiger. Power was supplied by a 260-cubic-inch Ford V-8 that gave sparkling performance.

Rootes (after whom the company was named) died, and within a couple of years, Chrysler was calling the shots at Rootes. This put the American automaker in an embarrassing position. Chrysler was selling a car equipped with an engine (as well as a guarantee) that came from its rival, Ford Motor Company. The obvious fix would be to install a Chrysler engine in the Tiger instead, but all of Chrysler's V-8s were too big to fit into the Tiger's small engine compartment.

An improved Tiger II was already in the works, and surprisingly, it went on sale as planned in 1967. The main change was the use of Ford's new 289-cubic-inch V-8 with 200 horsepower. Also added were an eggcrate grille insert, twin rocker-panel stripes, and revised badges reading "Sunbeam V-8" instead of "Powered by Ford 260." Britain's *Autocar* magazine reported a two-second improvement in the 0-60-mph time, now down to 7.5 seconds. Top speed went up only slightly, from 117 mph to 122 mph. The Tiger II was now the equal of Jaguar's E-Type sports car in acceleration (though not in top speed), and much quicker than anything offered by MG or Triumph.

But it didn't matter. Less than 600 Tiger IIs were built before the idea of selling a Ford-powered car finally hurt Chrysler's pride, so the Tiger II was discontinued during the 1967 model year. And some folks still haven't forgiven Chrysler for that.

SPECIFICATIONS

Engine type	Ford OHV V-8
Displacement	260 cid/4261 cc to 289 cid/ 4737 cc
Horsepower	164 @ 4400 rpm to 200 @ 4400 rpm
Transmission	4-speed manual
Suspension	independent front/live rear axle
Brakes	front discs/ rear drums
Wheelbase (in.)	86.0
Weight (lbs)	2560
Top speed (mph)	117-122
0-60 mph (sec)	7.5-9.5

This Mark II Tiger wears the optional hardtop. The Mark II used the larger Ford 289 V-8 that made it much faster than most competitors.

1985-1989 TOYOTA MR2

Japan's first mid-engine production car was greeted as one of the best sports cars around regardless of price. The fact that the MR2 comes from a company known mainly for its economy cars just makes it all the more amazing.

Like its American rival, the Pontiac Fiero, the MR2 (which means something like "Mid/Rear-engine 2-seater") is what might be described as a corporate kit car: a combination of mechanical pieces from various cars arranged in a new way. It's an idea as old as the first hot rod or, more recently, the Lotus Europa, Porsche 914, and Fiat X1/9. If the MR2 has any advantage here, it is probably because Toyota had some terrific pieces to pull off its shelves.

The idea for the MR2 was born in the late Seventies. A project team at Toyota began looking at the possibility of building a sports car using parts from the company's little front-wheel-drive Tercel. Later, Toyota redesigned its popular Corolla sedans to be front-wheel drive, and these components became the MR2's building blocks. A prototype was seen at various auto shows about a year ahead of the production MR2, which went on sale in Japan in June 1984 and arrived in the U.S. in February of '85.

There's nothing very unusual about the MR2's mechanical makeup. The four-cylinder engine and transaxle were lifted straight from the front-wheel drive Corolla. So were the brakes and suspension pieces. While a single overhead cam 1.5-liter engine powered the base Japanese model, all MR2s shipped to the U.S. have the double-overhead-cam 16-valve engine first seen in the rear-wheel-drive 1984 Corolla Sport coupes. Steering is rack and pinion *without* power assist; power steering is not really needed because of the light front end.

Most critics expressed disappointment with MR2 styling. Some considered it too plain and not that pretty, though many people would disagree. But in any case, beauty is only skin deep, and the MR2 has plenty of inner charm.

One of them is the snug but surprisingly comfortable cockpit. Unlike the "low-down, laid-back" driving position of the Fiero (which many find uncomfortable), the MR2 has a more normal, upright driving position, with well-placed pedals and

shifter. Everything is easy to reach, and body-hugging sports seats make racing through corners a joy. Also included are tilt steering wheel, AM/FM stereo radio, and power mirrors, while leather upholstery, alarm system, tilt/takeout glass sunroof, air conditioning, and power windows and door locks are optional. With reasonable base prices of $11,000-$14,000, it's easy to understand the MR2's instant sales success.

Comparisons between the MR2 and the Fiero are natural, since they are similar in concept, packaging, and marketing. Perhaps the best way to describe the difference is to say that the Toyota does more with less. Being much lighter than the Pontiac, the Toyota handles better and is easier to drive. Neither car is really quiet, a traditional mid-engine drawback, though both make nice noises.

But it's the twincam (double-

overhead-cam) engine that gives the MR2 so much of its charm and is, perhaps, its biggest advantage over the Fiero. Quite simply, this engine loves to rev—as indeed it must for best performance. But it's so smooth and willing and the shifter so quick and precise, that you feel like you're driving an honest-to-goodness race car. Few cars make their drivers look so good or smile so much.

Fortunately, the MR2 has been changed very little since its introduction. The '86 models offered several new options, including 4-speed automatic transmission, T-bar roof, and add-on spoilers. The '87s received larger rear brakes and minor cosmetic changes.

For 1988, however, a new model with a supercharged engine became available. Unlike a turbocharger, which is driven by exhaust gases, a supercharger is mechanically driven by the engine. Turbocharged engines generally need to be revved to higher speeds to make their best power. But with a supercharger, since the added power is available at lower speeds, it's easier to drive, especially in traffic.

The supercharger raised horsepower from 115 to 145, but numbers don't tell the whole story. Some drivers felt that some of the car's eager character had been diluted. Sure, the original engine was more work to drive, but the driver's effort was amply rewarded with delightful mechanical music.

Sales of the MR2 have slowed in the last couple of years. The market for two-seaters has always been small, and rising insurance rates complicate the sales picture even more. But Toyota, not content with its reputation for excellent quality and reliability, also wants to be known as a company that makes cars that are exciting and fun to drive. In the spring of 1990, a totally new MR2—larger and much smoother looking—will beckon to a new generation of enthusiasts.

SPECIFICATIONS

Engine type	DOHC inline-4
Displacement	97 cid/1587cc
Horsepower	112 @ 6600 rpm to 145 @ 6400 rpm
Transmission	5-speed manual or 4-speed automatic
Suspension	all independent
Brakes	front/rear discs
Wheelbase (in.)	91.3
Weight (lbs)	2290
Top speed (mph)	115-120
0-60 mph (sec)	8.5-9.0

Styling on the MR2 wasn't exactly graceful, but the car's eager character made up for it. The rear spoiler was optional. The MR2 was an instant sales success.

Power came from a 1.6-liter double-overhead-cam four-cylinder with 16 valves. For 1988, Toyota sped up the MR2 with a new supercharged version. Sales have declined in recent years as Americans cooled to two-seaters.

1969-1976 TRIUMPH TR6

Like MG, Triumph has been in the sports-car game for a long time. Though it began building automobiles as early as 1923, Triumph's first real sports car didn't come along until 30 years later. Called the TR2, it was a major turning point for Triumph.

Like the MG TC, it became popular in the U.S., and gained a loyal following. Compared to the MG, however, it seemed much more modern, and was also much faster, being able to top 100 mph.

Though it lasted only two years, the TR2 made quite a name for itself. The TR3 that followed showed few changes (the addition of front disc brakes being its major claim to fame), and likewise lasted but two years. Slightly modified versions called the TR3A and TR3B ran from 1958 to 1962, but again, nothing much was new.

The big news came in 1961 with the appearance of the TR4. Though TR3Bs were still being shipped to the U.S. when production first started, TR4s soon replaced them in the showrooms. Though the TR4 appeared to be an all-new car, its appearance was the only thing that was new. Mechanically, it was the same as the TR3 series. But instead of the TR3's sweeping fenders and "bugeye" headlights, the TR4 had a more modern, straight-line look. As might be expected, performance was unchanged.

But not for long. In 1965, the TR4A arrived, which was only slightly different on the outside, but very different underneath. The 2.2-liter four-cylinder engine remained, but power was up slightly, as was top speed—now almost 110 mph. The best news was that the old "live" rear axle (sometimes called a solid rear axle) was replaced by independent rear suspension. This greatly improved not only the handling, but also the ride, which had long been a sore point on the TRs.

Despite these improvements, however, the Triumphs were beginning to show their age. Other sports cars were coming along that offered better performance, and it was determined that the 2.2-liter four-cylinder engine (which had been used since 1962) was about as powerful as it would ever get. But that problem would soon be solved as well.

The TR5 that bowed in 1967 looked almost exactly like the TR4A, but was equipped with a 2.5-liter six-cylinder engine. But in order to meet coming U.S. emissions standards, Triumph decided to build two versions of the car: the TR5 for the European market, and the TR250 for the U.S.

On the surface, it looked as though the U.S. got the short end of the stick. The TR250's carbureted engine didn't

produce any more peak horsepower than the old four-cylinder engine (still at 104), although midrange power was better. This meant that the TR250 wasn't any faster than the old TR4A, but the engine was noticeably smoother, and made the car easier to drive at low speeds. The TR5, however, was another story. Equipped with fuel injection instead of carburetors, it produced 150 horsepower, which made the car a lot faster: 0-60 mph took but 8.8 seconds (versus 10.6 for the TR250), and top speed was raised to 120 mph. But the TR5 turned out to be a real gas guzzler, and the fuel-injection system was not as reliable as were the TR250's good old carburetors.

Surprisingly, the TR5/TR250 lasted less than two years. But by this time, styling was getting old, and many felt it was time for something new. And Triumph responded.

Enter the TR6. The mechanical pieces were changed little from the TR5/TR250, and even the body was basically the same, but new front fenders, hood, grill, and rear end gave it a much different look. The optional

The Triumph TR6 shown here has the optional hardtop in place. European models featured fuel injection, and were much faster than the carbureted versions sold in the U.S.

hardtop was also redesigned, becoming more angular in appearance. All in all, as facelifts go, this one was quite effective and handsome. In fact, many felt that the TR6 was the best-looking Triumph ever.

There were still two versions, fuel-injected European and carbureted American, but both were known simply as the TR6. U.S. models started out with the same 104 horsepower as the TR250, and Triumph managed to maintain that rating (even added a couple horses later on) in spite of ever-tightening U.S. emissions standards. The fuel-injected European engine also stayed at its former rating of 150 horsepower.

The TR6 would carry on for some seven years with few changes. A very small front "lip" spoiler was added in 1973, along with restyled dashboard gauges. Large black bumper guards at each end to meet America's new 5-mph impact-protection standards were fitted for '74.

This lack of change seems sad, but this was an aging design, and Triumph had plans to introduce a very different kind of sports car. Though the new car came out in the spring of 1975, TR6 production continued through July '76, although at a slower pace. As it turns out, the TR7 that followed would generate nowhere near as much affection as the beloved TR6.

SPECIFICATIONS

Engine type	OHV inline-6
Displacement	152.4 cid/ 2498 cc
Horsepower	104 @ 4900 rpm to 150 @ 5500 rpm
Transmission	4-speed manual (electric overdrive optional)
Suspension	all independent
Brakes	front/rear drums
Wheelbase (in.)	88.0
Weight (lbs)	2475
Top speed (mph)	119 (European model), 109 (U.S. version)
0-60 mph (sec)	8.2 (European model), 10.7 (U.S. version)

The TR6's long hood hides a 2.5-liter overhead-valve inline six-cylinder engine. The car shown here is in European trim with the fuel-injected engine.

1980-1990
TVR TASMIN FAMILY

Tiny English automaker TVR started out in 1958 building an odd-looking little sports car called the Grantura. It had a fiberglass coupe body fitted to a tubular chassis, and was powered by whatever engines TVR could get its hands on—mostly 4-cylinder Triumphs, MGs, and the like. But the first "real" TVR, called the Griffith, came out in 1963, and the history behind it is rather interesting.

In 1962, TVR entered three MG-powered Granturas in the 12-hour Sebring race. Two of the team drivers had their personal cars maintained at the same garage, owned by a man named Jack Griffith. One of these cars was a street-version Grantura; the other was a brand-new Shelby-Cobra. As the story goes, Griffith's mechanics decided one day to see whether the Cobra's mighty Ford V-8 could be squeezed into the tiny TVR's engine compartment. Amazingly enough, it fit, and the TVR Griffith was born.

Since the TVR weighed less than 2000 pounds, and the Ford V-8 put out 271 horsepower, the Griffith was outrageously quick. Zero-to-60 mph took 5.7 seconds, and top speed was over 150 mph. Needless to say, TVR's tiny sports car made quite a name for itself.

Unfortunately, workmanship was rather poor, and financial problems forced TVR to fold in 1965. But TVR was soon purchased by another company, and two years later, the Tuscan was introduced.

Initially built with only a four-cylinder engine, the Ford V-8 was later offered, but sales were low—less than 50 from 1967 to 1970. At one point, a V-6 version was added, and sales improved to 101 over a three-year period.

A new body and chassis arrived in 1972, but the car looked quite a bit like the earlier model. Called the M-series, it was offered only in four- and six-cylinder versions. However, one of the six-cylinder engines eventually got a turbocharger, and that brought horsepower up almost to V-8 levels. Another change was the addition of a convertible model in 1978, but by this time, a new design was on the drawing board.

TVR entered the Eighties with a new and very dramatic-looking replacement for the M-Series. Over the next several years, its chassis would carry small V-8s made by Rover (an English car company) as well as Ford V-6 engines, both manual and automatic transmissions, and convertible, coupe, and 2+2 body styles. Add in minor styling and model-name changes, and the story gets rather confusing. Models shipped to the U.S., however, are much easier to track; so far, all have had a German Ford 2.8-liter V-6 engine, and most have been convertibles.

Despite all the differences, these TVRs shared two traits. First, they're true sports cars in the great British tradition. Second, they're the best-built TVRs ever.

The first of the breed appeared in January 1980: a wedge-shaped two-seat hatchback coupe called the Tasmin. A 2+2 version (having a small back seat) and convertible came soon after.

Though its design was new, the Tasmin stuck with TVR's usual construction and layout. Its chassis was basically the same "space frame" used on the M-Series, made up of small-diameter tubes. All-independent coil-spring suspension and rack-and-pinion steering were also carried over, but disc brakes were now used at the rear as well as at the front. As before, bodies were made of fiberglass, and major components like engines, transmissions, and differentials were purchased from larger automakers.

Styling was where the Tasmin changed the most. Here was the first TVR that could honestly be called handsome instead of "distinctive" (a word often used by auto journalists as a nice way of saying ugly). The clean, sharp-edged styling might be a little dated for the Eighties (since smooth, rounded shapes are now in fashion), but it's a vast improvement over previous TVRs. In some ways, it looks rather like a late-model Lotus, but the long hood (necessary because the whole engine sits behind the front wheels) gives it an entirely different profile.

The primary engine used during the Tasmin's first four years was the fuel-injected version of Ford's 2.8-liter OHV V-6. Since this engine had already been "de-smogged" to meet U.S. emissions standards, TVR was once again able to sell cars in the U.S. With about 145 horsepower, the Tasmin could run up to 125 mph flat out.

Meanwhile, TVR was once again purchased by another company. The new owners wanted to improve performance, so various engine swaps were tried. After testing a turbo V-6 (two prototypes were built) the company settled on Rover's all-aluminum 3.5-liter V-8 engine, which in its latest fuel-injected form delivered 190 bhp.

By 1984, the V-6 Tasmin had been renamed 280i and the new V-8, called 350i, was on the road. The 350i was a true supercar, with top speeds in the 135-140-mph range and acceleration to match.

But it was only a first step. Late '84 brought the 390SE, a 3.9-liter version of the V-8 delivering upwards of 250 horsepower. Styling was smoothed out a little for 1986, when the even hotter 420SEAC arrived. With about 300 horsepower from its 4.2-liter V-8, the 420SEAC had a top speed in excess of 150 mph.

While styling and quality have improved greatly since that big Ford V-8 was wedged into the tiny little Griffith over 25 years ago, performance is remarkably similar. While today's TVR has come a long way from those early models, they are a welcome addition to the growing ranks of high-performance cars that will take us into the Nineties.

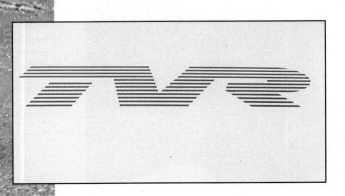

The TVR Tasmin pictured here is a 1985 280i model with a fuel-injected Ford 2.8-liter V-6. The car is available as a coupe or convertible in two-seater and 2+2 versions. Engines range from the Ford V-6 to one of two Rover V-8 engines.

SPECIFICATIONS

Engine type	OHV V-6/OHV V-8
Displacement	170 cid/2792 cc to 258 cid/ 4228 cc
Horsepower	160 @ 5700 rpm to 300 @ 5500 rpm
Transmission	4- and 5-speed manual or 3-speed automatic
Suspension	all independent
Brakes	front discs/ rear drums
Wheelbase (in.)	94.0
Weight (lbs)	2365-2535
Top speed (mph)	108-150+
0-60 mph (sec)	5.6-11.8

Though rounded styling may be more fashionable, the Tasmin's sharp-edged look is still modern and up to date.